Y0-CBK-427

GREAT DETECTIVES

Eugène François Vidocq
Allan Pinkerton
Alphonse Bertillon
Marie-François Goron
John Wilson Murray
Sir Bernard Spilsbury
Arthur Fowler Neil
Elmer Lincoln Irey
John Edgar Hoover
Raymond Campbell Schindler
Robert Fabian
United States Bureau of Narcotics

GREAT

Famous real-life

Robert Liston

Platt & Munk, Publishers
New York

DETECTIVES

sleuths and their most baffling cases

To Cindy, Stephen, Felicia . . . mysteries all

ACKNOWLEDGMENTS

Most grateful thanks go to individuals who helped with this book: Bernard Garfinkel, my editor; the staffs of the New York, Boston, and Westport and Norwalk, Connecticut, libraries, who assisted with the research; Henry Schneider, an excellent spokesman for United States Treasury agents; and Clyde Newstrand, the laying of whose garage floor turned out to be helpful.

CONTENTS

EUGÈNE
FRANÇOIS
VIDOCQ

 |||||

Magician of disguise

† A truly black night it was, moonless, starless, with heavy rain-sodden clouds hanging low over the ground—hardly a fit night for any man to be out-of-doors anywhere in France, let alone on the roads near Paris in the mid-1820's.

For months travelers had been terrorized by highwaymen, brigands, robbers and thieves of various persuasions who clubbed, stabbed, shot and robbed, then asked questions later. All of Paris was alarmed about the situation —but not Fontaine the butcher. A fat, jovial, and obviously none too bright individual, he was journeying to his home at Courtille after attending a fair near Corbeil.

Walking alone, Fontaine stopped at an inn near Essonne for some food and a liter of wine. His spirits soaring, he made friends with three men who told him they, too, were traveling to Courtille. Why didn't they go together? It seemed a good idea to Fontaine, especially—as he said—since he was carrying fifteen hundred francs. One couldn't have too much protection, could one?

So Fontaine, either drunk or incredibly naive, started out with his "bodyguards," a happy quartet, laughing, chortling, singing bawdy songs in raucous voices not even a cold shower deserved. Then, near a crossroads where the whole universe seemed to be windswept emptiness, Fontaine was clubbed on the head from the rear. He lurched under the blow and staggered to one knee. A second blow crashed into his skull, and he toppled to the roadway. One of his companions bent over him to lift his purse.

What Fontaine lacked in brains he made up in girth. More than two good whacks on the head were needed to keep him down. With a scream of rage, he kicked his attacker, rolled to his feet and took on all three men. He put up a worthy struggle, kicking and shoving and clawing amid great grunts and horrendous bellows.

But Fontaine, for all his courage, was no match for the knife plunged into his side. He doubled over and fell backward as the second knife thrust pushed him to the ground. He was defenseless as the assailant leaped atop him and again and again thrust the knife home— twenty-eight times in all. His purse taken, Fontaine was left for dead.

Incredibly he wasn't. Perhaps it was his fat that saved him, or the darkness and poor aim of the knifer, but after a few minutes of unconsciousness he came around, at least enough to moan and cry feebly for help. Fortunately, his cries were heard by another traveler, and he was taken into Corbeil where, to the astonishment of all, he did not die.

The local prosecutor quickly came to question Fontaine, who, despite his pain, was able to gasp out a brief description of his assailants. The prosecutor visited the scene of the crime and studied it carefully. He also did a very smart thing, for those days, by collecting various items found at the scene, including several buttons, fragments of cloth and some blood-stained pieces of paper. He even made impressions of footprints, figuring all of this might be usable as evidence—in case the footpads were ever caught.

The prosecutor realized, however, that for all his efforts he had no more chance of apprehending the bandits than poor Fontaine had. But he knew of someone who could—and perhaps even put an end to the reign of terror on the roads near Paris. Thus, he sent for Vidocq.

A legend in his own time and ever since, Eugène François Vidocq was the world's first professional detective. He was also perhaps the best detective the world has ever produced. No man before or since has had the knowledge of crime and criminals that Vidocq possessed or his courage, cleverness, resourcefulness, talent for deception and just plain daring, all of which were needed to catch Fontaine's attackers.

Certainly there have been far cleverer criminals than those sought by Vidocq. The science of crime and of crime detection has advanced a thousandfold since the gritty little French detective worked his wonders. But for his day and age, Vidocq's accomplishments were wonders. He had no knowledge of fingerprint identification, no photography, no crime lab to turn blood spots into evidence and loose threads into a hangman's rope. Vidocq operated without cars, radio, telephone or telegraph. In fact, just about all he had were his wits—and courage.

Vidocq's contribution to law and order is immeasureable. Police who today hire paid informers, who send an undercover agent to infiltrate a gang, who use make-up or disguises to impersonate another man are only imitating techniques originated by Vidocq. The thin-faced, dark-eyed Frenchman was the first to use psychological techniques to extract confessions, the first to keep systematic crime records, the first to study criminals and to use their own methods against them, the first to organize a detective force to work full time at solving crimes. The technique of detection using seemingly insignificant clues began with Vidocq.

When the public prosecutor at Corbeil thought to call Vidocq to rid his territory of highwaymen, it was proof of how far Vidocq had come. He was born in Arras, France, on July 23, 1775, next door to the house where the infamous Robespierre, the butcher of the French Revolution, had been born sixteen years earlier. Vidocq's father was a baker and a heavy-handed disciplinarian against whom Vidocq rebelled. At an early age he ran away from home and into a life of almost constant adventure. He became a showman, soldier, sailor, puppet master, and general ne'er-do-well.

His was the time of the French Revolution, when decadent royalty was swept away to be replaced by violence, bloodshed and anarchy. Peasants, long oppressed by the Kings of France, relieved their frustration by pillage and the guillotine. Then came Napoleon and iron discipline and war and greatness and, finally, defeat.

Vidocq was a part of all this. If life was hard, so was justice. The death penalty was meted out for seemingly insignificant offenses, and if there was any doubt about a man's guilt there was always life imprisonment at hard labor. Freedom was worth dying for, but the concept of civil liberties was wasted on the illiterate. Thus, Vidocq, while still in his early twenties, found himself thrown into jail for beating up an officer who had stolen one of his girl friends. He escaped, was recaptured and escaped again. He was put in the chain gang at hard labor—and escaped again.

Admiration for the clever escape artist mounted among France's sizable army of convicts, and in their grimy dungeons they recounted how he escaped from prison in a policeman's stolen uniform or how he leaped from a prison tower to a river below.

The last escape was in 1799, and Vidocq seemingly made it good, living in Paris as an old-clothes dealer. But his was a life of incessant fear. Ex-convicts and old comrades constantly threatened to betray him unless he helped or sheltered them.

After ten years of being preyed upon by the underworld, Vidocq, in despair and anger, went to the police and offered to turn informer. His timing was excellent, for Monsieur Henri, the Paris Prefect (Chief) of Police, was struggling to stem the tide of crime sweeping Paris in 1810. But with twenty-eight justices of the peace and a handful of inspectors, his task seemed hopeless.

Aware that an informer in criminal ranks could be invaluable, Henri accepted Vidocq's offer and arranged to have him "re-captured" and sent to La Force prison, where the worst criminals were kept. Vidocq was welcomed as a criminal celebrity and taken into the confidence of prisoners on whom he secretly informed for the next twenty-two months. Then, while being "transferred" to the chain gang, Vidocq "escaped."

He went to Paris, where he organized the Brigade de Sûreté, as the detective force of the French police is called today. With first four, then twelve, and ultimately twenty ex-convicts as his detectives, he warred on crime.

For a long time he posed as a criminal, infiltrating many gangs. But eventually the Parisian underworld learned of his true activities, and he became marked for an early and preferably tortured death. Then Vidocq developed the techniques which made him famous. He became a man of a thousand faces. A change of clothing, a little make-up, an alteration in his voice and he was a thief, forger, mugger or worse. He walked into incredible danger, armed only with his wits and daring. All France was agog at his exploits.

Vidocq personally arrested thousands of people and developed a fantastic memory for names, faces, voices, dates, crimes—information which he used to identify criminals.

All of Vidocq's talents were called into service to capture Fontaine's assailants. When he arrived at Corbeil, Vidocq looked over the evidence gathered by the prosecutor, then congratulated him on his thoroughness. Most intriguing was a torn piece of paper which the assailant had obviously used to wipe his knife clean. At the top of the sheet, severed by the tear in the paper, was part of an address:

> *To Monsieur Rao—*
> *Wine Merchant*
> *Bar— Roche—*
> *Cli—*

Vidocq thought about that fragment of an address for several days. He had no way of figuring out the name, but from his intimate knowledge of Paris and its environs, he decided the address had to be this:

> *To Monsieur* _____, *Wine Merchant*
> *Barrier Rochechouart*
> *Chausée (Road) de Clignancourt*

Vidocq's guess was that the wine merchant either knew of the highwaymen or may have been one of them. So he and his men began to make exhaustive inquiries about the wine merchant. They quickly learned he was Clair Raoul, a man whose reputation left something to be desired. He was rather tough and brutal, and his tavern was a hangout for unsavory characters. Raoul and his friends frequently left the tavern early at night, returning in the morning tired and covered with mud. All of this led Vidocq to look upon Raoul as a "finished criminal," as he termed him.

Meanwhile, Vidocq's men were tracing Raoul's companions, and they discovered a man fitting the description of one of Fontaine's assailants. Vidocq joined a stake-out of this new suspect's house. All night and all day until four o'clock the next afternoon he waited, in growing exasperation.

Suddenly the suspect appeared, and Vidocq recognized him at once as Court, a man he had arrested years before for robbery. But there was something strange about him. Yes, he was limping. Vidocq recalled Fontaine's saying that during the struggle, one of his assailants had fallen to his knees and cried out in pain.

On the basis of the description, the limp and Court's criminal past, Vidocq made him a major suspect and decided to gamble that he had the right man. He went to Court's door and knocked.

"Who's there?" asked Court.

"It's Raoul," said Vidocq, imitating the wine merchant.

"Is there something new?" asked Court, obviously hesitant about showing himself.

"Yes, there is something new."

With that Court, his wife at his side, opened the door and recognized Vidocq. "Oh, it's Monsieur Jules," as Vidocq was known throughout the underworld.

"Monsieur Jules!" exclaimed Court's wife, and she shrank back into the house in fright.

"What of it?" said Vidocq, grinning. "I'm not the devil."

Court hesitated a moment, then, endeavoring to smile broadly, said, "That's right. Monsieur Jules arrested me once, but I'm not sore."

Vidocq entered, and there was some reasonably civil conversation in which the detective spoke of some trouble and the need to question Court. Without actually saying so, he hinted at a charge of smuggling, which was heatedly—and honestly—denied by Court. Nevertheless, said Vidocq, Court would have to come along to the station while the matter was cleared up. Perhaps it would be better if Court's wife came, too.

All of this, terribly illegal by today's standards of criminal procedure, was a necessity for Vidocq. He couldn't allow Court to get away. Hiding out was easy in those days of poor transportation and worse communication. If Court believed the police were after him for any crime, no matter what, he'd simply disappear. A change of name and address, a new beard and occupation, and the chances of anyone recognizing him would be quite small. Vidocq felt he had to arrest Court on some trumped-up charge to keep him from running away. Similarly, he had to arrest Court's wife, because she would go straight to Raoul, warn him of Court's arrest, and he, too, would take off.

With Court and his wife safely in jail, Vidocq tackled the problem of Raoul. He went to his tavern, but Raoul was gone. No one seemed to know where. In mounting desperation, Vidocq waited, afraid the suspect had fled. Then, in the afternoon, Raoul appeared, greeting the detective cordially, if somewhat warily.

Vidocq played to the hilt the part of the reluctant policeman. "I am disturbed," he said sorrowfully, "to have such a disagreeable mission. If I'd known it was you involved in this matter, Raoul, I'd have excused myself."

There were some more apologies punctuated with deep sighs. Raoul, thoroughly perplexed, interrupted to ask what the detective's onerous task was.

Vidocq was so long-faced that he appeared on the verge of tears. It seemed, he said, that the political authorities had learned of some men, suspected of disloyalty to the Republic, who were gathering to sing slanderous songs in Raoul's tavern.

"I didn't know politics was your department," said

Raoul, delighted to have the detective in an embarrassing position.

Vidocq shrugged and looked pained. "When one is in the shop, he has to do a little of everything."

Then Vidocq suggested that if Raoul would just turn over the seditious songs to him and not allow the singers in his restaurant any more, the entire matter could be forgotten. He, Vidocq, would leave him in peace.

When Raoul insisted the whole charge was poppy-cock, Vidocq suggested that he be allowed to search Raoul's home as proof. Raoul agreed, but first, he said, he had to cut the meat to be served at the tavern.

"Fine," said Vidocq, "I'll help you," and for the next five hours, rather than let Raoul out of his sight, Vidocq acted as second cook, cutting veal and lamb for stew and mixing wines which sold for six sous a liter. As Raoul swung the meat cleaver, Vidocq knew that, should he become suspicious, he would not hesitate to separate one nosy detective's ears.

Eventually, Raoul and Vidocq, accompanied by two of his men, went to Raoul's Paris apartment to search for the "slanderous songs." They went through drawers and closets, and finally Vidocq asked if he could look in Raoul's writing desk. After that the detectives would leave. The desk was opened, and amid the papers Vidocq spotted the tell-tale stationery with its letterhead. There was even one torn sheet which matched perfectly the blood-stained paper found at the scene of the attack on Fontaine.

At that instant Raoul realized he had been tricked and leaped for a brace of pistols hidden in a drawer. But Vidocq and his men were quicker. Raoul was arrested and taken to jail, but he was kept separated from Court.

Vidocq now had two suspects, but not much more than suspicion to go on. He certainly lacked proof that they had been anywhere near Corbeil or the inn at Essonne. Now, if he could just get a confession. . . .

Vidocq went to work on Court first. Pretending to know vastly more than he did, he hinted at knowledge of murders. "Believe me," he said with exaggerated sincerity, "tell the truth. Why persist in hiding what we already know? All the people you have attacked aren't dead. They'll testify against you, and if you persist in lying, the magistrate will give you no peace. You'll go to prison and it'll be hell for you. On the other hand, if you are truly repentant, the judge may take pity on you and . . . who knows? You may get off easy."

Vidocq went on like this until Court, thoroughly convinced he was trapped, confessed—to the murder of a poultry dealer of which Vidocq knew absolutely nothing. "The poor devil," said Court, "to recover from such an assault."

Vidocq, struggling to keep from laughing at this turn of events, said, "What of the butcher—the one you riddled with your knife?"

Court seemed surprised. "Him? May God have his soul. If he testifies against me, it will be at the Last Judgment."

"You're wrong, my friend. The butcher didn't die."

Court was so shaken by the knowledge that anyone could have survived such a knife attack that he confessed and, after more questioning, admitted Raoul was his accomplice.

The detective next went to Raoul's cell while he was asleep and tried a little nineteenth-century subliminal suggestion. Bending over him, he whispered in his ear, "What became of the knife with which you murdered your victim?" Raoul awoke with a start but collected himself in time to deny any knowledge of any murders.

"Court confessed. You might as well," said Vidocq, careful not to say what Court had confessed to.

Raoul insisted he was innocent, so Vidocq brought the two suspects face to face. Court beamed and blurted, "I'm glad to hear you have followed my example and made a full confession." That broke it for Raoul, and he too confessed to murdering the poultry dealer and assaulting Fontaine.

The pair went before Fontaine, who identified them

as his attackers, and they were returned to prison to await trial. But Vidocq still wanted to identify the third member of the gang. He visited Court and Raoul in their cell. As he questioned them, an elaborate dinner was brought in for the three of them, complete with an abundance of wine. To show how much he trusted them, Vidocq even allowed them to have knives to cut their meat.

As the wine took effect, Vidocq talked about the robberies and how smart they were to confess. He said he was continuing his investigation. "Several people have said there were at least four of you on your expeditions."

"No, no," said Raoul, "they're wrong. On my word, Monsieur Jules, we never had more than three. The other is a former lieutenant in the customs, Pons Gerard."

Raoul described Gerard as a formidable individual with the "strength of ten" and warned Vidocq not to tangle with him. "You should find some way to take him when he's asleep," said Raoul.

And Court added, with a wicked grin, "But he rarely sleeps."

Gerard lived in the village of La Capelle in the district of Aisne, and it was there that Vidocq, disguised as a horse dealer, went to find him. Accompanying him, pretending to be grooms, were Detectives Goury and Clement.

Everyone at La Capelle knew Gerard—and feared

him, for he was a huge man of prodigious strength and monumental distemper. Even the authorities were afraid of him. So it was not without some hesitation that Vidocq went to the tavern Gerard frequently visited. Posing as a friend of Gerard's, he got the proprietress to tell him where the big man could be found.

The trail led to a road at the edge of town where Gerard, who apparently held some kind of minor village office, was superintending a crew of about three hundred men making road repairs. From a distance, Vidocq decided that he and his two men might stand a chance of overpowering the hulking Gerard, but if the thirty workmen aided their leader—well, it did make one shudder.

Again the detective chose to let his wits do what brawn could not. Without hesitation he went up to Gerard and, grinning and extending a hand, said, "Bonjour, Pons, how are you?"

Gerard scowled suspiciously and in the style of speech of the day said, "The devil take me if I know you. Who are you?"

"What! You don't recognize me. I must have changed."

Gerard blinked and peered at Vidocq even more intently. "No, I don't know you. What's your name?"

Vidocq leaned close to Gerard and whispered in his ear, "I'm a friend of Court and Raoul. They sent me."

"Oh-h, of course," said Gerard, beaming and pressing Vidocq's hand. "I must have a short memory. Of course it's you. Imagine me not knowing a friend like you." Yet Gerard still had reservations and asked about Vidocq's two men.

"My grooms," said the detective.

"I did not doubt it, not for a minute I didn't. Well—" he patted his belly. "Come, have a drink—and bring your grooms."

At the friendly neighborhood tavern Vidocq explained that he had been lunching with Raoul and Court when the police arrived and arrested all three of them for the attack on the butcher. The police had quickly realized their mistake and let him go. Now he had come to La Capelle at the request of Court and Raoul to warn him.

After expressing his eternal gratitude, Gerard asked, "Who arrested Raoul and Court?"

"Vidocq."

"Oh, that blackguard," Gerard roared. "I don't know him, but I would willingly pay several bottles of good wine to anyone who would show him to me."

"It's not hard to meet him. He's always rambling about."

"He'd better not fool with me," growled Gerard. "If he were here, I'd give him a bad hour or two."

Vidocq laughed. "You're just like the rest. You talk of

what you'd do, and yet if he were before you at this moment, you'd be the first to offer him a glass of wine."

With that Vidocq held out his glass.

"I!" snorted Gerard, filling Vidocq's glass. "I offer him wine! May a thousand devils seize me first!"

Vidocq leaped to his feet. "Yes, you! I say you would want him to drink with you."

"I tell you I would die sooner!"

"Then," said Vidocq with an immense grin, "you may die as soon as you please, for *I* am Vidocq and I arrest you."

Handcuffs were clasped on the speechless Gerard, and he was tried beside his accomplices. Raoul and Court got the guillotine for murdering the poultry dealer. Gerard, who could not be implicated in that crime, received life imprisonment for assaulting Fontaine.

The Fontaine case was far from the most dangerous or colorful that Vidocq ever solved, but it best illustrates the various methods he pioneered. Use of clues, psychology to obtain confessions, surveillance, undercover work, patience, boldness—all these are still the hallmarks of a good detective. Perhaps no detective today has the memory, daring and resourcefulness of Vidocq. Such advances as fingerprinting, communication and crime labs have reduced the need for memories and methods as fantastic as those of the original detective. Nor could today's detective possess Vidocq's intimate knowledge of crime, because no habitual criminal and ex-con, as Vidocq was for the first thirty-five years of his life, could serve on a police force.

Vidocq was not able to be a cop for long. In 1828 he was forced to resign when a new prefect of police objected to having his entire detective bureau staffed by ex-convicts. He did have a point there.

Vidocq then wrote his memoirs, which were printed and translated all over the world. Then he opened a paper mill, but this was unsuccessful. Next he formed the world's first private detective agency and was immensely successful. Then—some say because of police jealousy—he was arrested on a charge of "betraying confidence." He was acquitted, arrested again, convicted, but released on appeal.

These actions, plus numerous lawsuits, wiped out his fortune. He spent his last years lecturing on his experiences and died in 1857, penniless. But, surely, the world has rarely seen a more remarkable criminologist—or a man who led a more fascinating life—than Vidocq, first among the master detectives.

ALLAN
PINKERTON

Scourge of western badmen

† He was, seemingly, a man without distinction. His clothes were unkempt and a ludicrous fit. His eyes seemed too shrewd, his nose overly long and his coarse black beard incapable of maintaining a trim. With his pronounced Scots burr, roughened hands and often coarse manners, he seemed an individual with a small destiny.

Seldom have appearances been more deceiving. Few men have accomplished more in their lifetimes or had a greater impact on history than Allan Pinkerton—the man described above, who was one of the great detectives of modern times. Founder of the Pinkerton National Detective Agency, the first successful private police force, Allan Pinkerton brought to the profession a respectability which has lasted to this day. In fact the word "Pinkerton" has almost entered the language as a noun synonymous with protection of private property and other valuables. But Pinkerton did far more than establish a profession. Among his many accomplishments as a detective, he broke up a plot to assassinate Abraham Lincoln. During the Civil War, he set up the United States Secret Service and made important contributions to modern techniques of spying.

But perhaps Pinkerton's greatest accomplishment was the role he played in the settlement of the West. Pinkertons were the principal, often the only, means of law enforcement west of the Mississippi River from the Civil War to the turn of the century. They protected shipments of mail and money, banks, stores and other commercial establishments throughout the West. They were not always successful. But it was Pinkerton and his detectives who tracked down the James Brothers, the Younger Brothers, the Farringtons, Burrows, Cooks, the Wild Bunch and other outlaw gangs that threatened to turn the West into a jungle. Pinkerton's work permitted the West to be opened to peaceful settlement, to become a place where money and not the "six gun" could be used to settle debts.

Pinkerton thus had tremendous impact not only on law enforcement, but on America's national development.

Most accounts of Pinkerton tend to lose sight of the man himself in recording his exciting deeds. Pinkerton's derring-do was remarkable, but so was the man.

Born in Gothals, Scotland, in 1819, Allan Pinkerton was, as a boy, plunged into the great social issue of his time. England's industrial revolution had created a new laboring class, who demanded an end to feudal-type monarchy and the initiation of electoral reform. The movement eventually became known as Chartism, a word that soon came to mean violence. Chartist mobs carried their frustrations into the street, where in 1829 Pinkerton's father, a police sergeant, was crippled for life as he tried to maintain order in the face of a howling mob. When the beaten and bloody elder Pinkerton was brought home, it was ten-year-old Allan who opened the door.

The fury of the Chartist mob affected Pinkerton's whole life, but in strange ways. It cut short any chance for an education he might have had. He left school and was apprenticed to a coopersmith so that he could help to support the family. The sight of his injured father gave him a lifelong regard for the need for law and order. Yet, strangely, he eventually became a Chartist and a participant in the very riots that had caused his father's injuries.

The time in which he grew up and the tragic events which affected his life gave Pinkerton a peculiar ambivalence. As a policeman's son he had a great belief in the need for law and order and the danger of mob rule. Yet he had great sympathy for the underprivileged, the oppressed, the helpless. This combination of authoritarianism and humanitarianism would show up repeatedly throughout his life.

In 1842 Pinkerton left for the New World with his bride. After a shipwreck and some other misadventures, Pinkerton and his wife ended up in Chicago, at that time a small, bustling, "wide-open" frontier town. Pinkerton began to work as a barrel-maker, eventually moving his family to Dundee, Illinois, located thirty-eight miles to the northwest of Chicago on the Fox River, where he operated his own cooperage firm and began to prosper, gaining the respect of the village for his thrift and hard work.

Pinkerton the humanitarian took time from business to join the Abolitionist movement. He was a supporter of John Brown, who led the raid at Harper's Ferry, and he ran an important way station on the "underground railway," which spirited runaway slaves North to freedom.

Yet the "cop" in Pinkerton was soon to make its appearance. A year or so after he arrived in Dundee, Pinkerton rowed to a small uninhabited island in the Fox River to search for suitable trees to cut into barrel staves. Instead he found something that would change his whole life: evidence that the island was being used by counterfeiters or "coiners," whose activities had plagued merchants in the area for months. A few nights later, Pinkerton joined the sheriff in capturing the gang. He was soon aiding the sheriff in other investigations and was finally named a deputy sheriff. Before long, merchants were hiring him to recover stolen property and to protect their valuables. So successful was Pinkerton that he gave up the cooperage business in 1850 and opened his detective agency.

It was a financial success from the beginning. In the settlement of the West, the building of railroads, the rapid expansion of commerce and the vast movement of goods and people raced far ahead of the ability to provide adequate police protection. There was a great need for a private police force—and Pinkerton filled the bill admirably.

His success was no accident, however. When he founded his agency, he formulated some very sound "general principles." No Pinkerton employee could accept a reward for his services. "Stool pigeons" (as they would be called today) or liquor could never be used to obtain a confession. Criminals must be treated fairly and be helped to become useful members of society. He decreed that his agency would never accept a divorce case, that evidence would never be "faked" and that charges should be on a *per diem* basis, so a client could always know what his costs would be. These high standards gave Pinkerton's agency a reputation for integrity and honesty, and businessmen were soon standing in line for his services.

More than integrity, however, is needed to make a good detective agency. Pinkerton personally selected and trained his men—and women—gathering a group of excellent people at a time when police forces were largely staffed with incompetents. But the biggest innovation Pinkerton brought to police work was teamwork. The master detective Vidocq had solved crimes personally with the use of a few "assistants." Pinkerton sent groups of men to work together in solving a case. Even on cases in which Pinkerton himself was involved in a most personal way, he never worked alone, but in close coordination with his men. He was simply "first among equals"—and this may have been his most lasting contribution to the art of detection.

As a detective, Pinkerton had an uncanny ability to be at the right spot at the right time. This quality showed up in 1861 when Lincoln was elected President. Lincoln and Pinkerton were both from Illinois and knew each other personally. When it was learned that an attempt would be made on the President-elect's life, Pinkerton was employed to stop it.

Early in 1861 Lincoln started east by train from Illinois, bound for his inauguration in Washington. His was a lengthy journey, both in time and in distance, for he was to make many stops to deliver major addresses along the way. Pinkerton and one of his men went to Baltimore, then a hotbed of secessionism. They infiltrated the organization of assassins and discovered that the plan was to attack Lincoln as he journeyed from Philadelphia to Washington. When Lincoln changed trains in Baltimore, the plotters intended to assault and murder him, secure in their knowledge that he traveled totally without guards.

Pinkerton arranged for Lincoln to take a different train and to sleep as an ordinary Pullman passenger in a car which was transferred, its precious cargo included, to the new train. Pinkerton also arranged to have the telegraph line cut between Philadelphia and Baltimore, so that the assassins in the Maryland city would be unable to learn of Lincoln's unscheduled departure. The result of Pinkerton's actions was that the attempted assassination never took place.

During the Civil War Pinkerton established the federal Secret Service, which engaged in considerable espionage across Confederate lines. This spying was not entirely successful, and Pinkerton's influence waned in the later stages of the war. He always regretted this, feeling that if he had been allowed to continue his activities, he could have prevented the death of Lincoln in 1865.

About a year and a half after that tragic event, Pinkerton became embroiled in one of his most famous cases. This case involved a brand-new crime—train robbery, as well as a new criminal technique—outlaws using trains to accomplish wide-ranging, fast-moving banditry. It also involved a new means of "law enforcement"—citizen "vigilantes," who took the law into their own hands. Though he was able to catch the celebrated Western badmen, the Reno Brothers, Pinkerton's work in this case turned out to be a numbing failure, particularly for a man whose life had been scarred by mob violence. As long as he lived, Pinkerton would remember the Reno case with sorrow.

The event which brought Pinkerton into the case occurred on October 6, 1866. It was late afternoon as an Ohio and Mississippi Railroad passenger train slowly chugged through southeastern Indiana. Many of the passengers, bored with the flat, familiar terrain, dozed off.

A few miles out of the town of Seymour, John Reno, his brother Simeon Reno and Franklin Sparks roused themselves and nonchalantly went, one by one, to the platform at the rear of the coach. No one paid much attention. They appeared to be getting a little fresh air and taking in the scenery, such as it was.

But the Reno brothers and Sparks were hardly intent on the beauties of nature. They were studying the Adams Express Company car which was next on the train. After exchanging a few last-minute words, they burst through the door of the express car, surprising the messenger at his desk. "I'll take this," said John Reno as he scooped up ten thousand dollars and put it in his pocket.

At the same time, one of the other men pulled the brake cord, opening the side door of the car as the train ground to a stop. The Renos and Sparks shoved the unopened safe to the ground and jumped out after it. They ran to the locomotive, threatened the engineer with their guns and forced him to chug away.

A posse sent out from the next town arrived on handcars before the bandits opened the safe, but the Reno brothers and Sparks escaped with the ten thousand dollars in America's first recorded train robbery.

Allan Pinkerton was hired by the Adams Company to

investigate the crime. The situation he found in Seymour, Indiana, was unlike any he had ever seen. Lost, confused, violence-crazed veterans of the Civil War had gathered in Seymour, along with deserters, criminals and plain thugs, to ride under the banner of the Reno brothers. There were five brothers, Frank, John, Simeon, Clinton and William, along with a sister, Laura Ellen, a respectable woman. Clinton refused to become an outlaw, but the other four brothers more than made up for the "defection" of the one "Honest Reno."

Even as young men the four Renos were unruly and lawbreakers. Before the War they burned down the entire town of Rockford, Indiana, forcing all its residents to move to Seymour—then bought the devastated area for $600.97, making the fire-scarred buildings their headquarters. Lawlessness swept Seymour. The sheriff, judges and prosecutors were all bribed by the Renos, and the town was, as the local newspaper put it, "a carnival of crime."

Pinkerton's quick examination of the Seymour situation told him he had no chance to arrest or convict the Renos for the train robbery. A more patient approach was needed and, thus, Seymour soon had another saloon. Its bartender was Dick Winscott, a big jovial man—and a Pinkerton operative. He got along famously with the Renos, so well in fact that he persuaded John and Frank

Reno, one drunken night, "to sit on stools with their beer glasses and pose for a picture." Intoxicated, they failed to notice that Winscott kept the pictures—which soon circulated among Pinkerton's men.

Pinkerton struck soon afterward. He arranged for Winscott to lure John Reno, leader of the gang, to the Seymour train depot on a pretext. Then Pinkerton arrived with six men on a special two-car train. They jumped from a still-moving car, grabbed Reno and pulled him, struggling and kicking, onto the train. Pinkerton waved to the engineer, and the locomotive raced for Cincinnati.

The remaining Renos commandeered a train and tried to rescue their brother, but they never could catch Pinkerton. John Reno was tried for robbery and sentenced to twenty-five years in the Missouri Penitentiary at Jefferson. At every step leading to prison, he expected to be freed by his brothers, and Pinkerton anticipated that they would try. But on January 18, 1868, he went behind bars —a most fortunate development for him.

A few weeks later at Marshfield, fourteen miles south of Seymour, a Jefferson, Missouri & Indianapolis Railroad train stopped about 11:00 P.M. to take on water and wood, necessary ingredients for locomotives at that time. As one of the firemen bent over to oil a locomotive driving rod, he was slugged on the head with a pistol butt.

Two other firemen rushed in to help and met a similar fate. Engineer George Fletcher climbed down from the cab to see what was going on, and he was knocked unconscious.

Then the Reno gang, in perhaps its most efficient robbery, swung into action. The Adams Express car was uncoupled from the coaches. With one of the Renos manning the throttle, the train raced off into the night. But only after the train conductor, who made a futile effort to stop the theft, was gunned down.

As the train rolled on, the outlaws crawled along the roof of the express car and dropped to the platform. Forcing the door, they burst in and pistol-whipped the messenger. An outlaw opened the side door, and the messenger was rolled out of the moving train. Fortunately he wasn't killed.

Leisurely the Renos opened the safe. Six miles south of Seymour they abandoned the train and rode off on horses—with ninety-six thousand dollars in gold and government bonds. The next day the outlaws split up. Frank Reno and four others went to Windsor, Canada. Simeon and William Reno went into hiding in Indianapolis.

The remaining members of the gang, including Franklin Sparks and John J. Moore, decided that one successful robbery deserved another. They selected a train and then proposed to its engineer that he join the gang. After consulting with Pinkerton, the engineer agreed to "help" them. Soon he told them of a run on which the train would be transporting a hundred thousand dollars in gold.

This robbery began in much the same fashion as the Marshfield robbery. The outlaws seized the train after it had stopped for fueling at Brownstown, six miles west of Seymour. The firemen were knocked out, and the engineer, by prior arrangement, was tied up and tossed in the cab. A few minutes later, as Moore burst into the express car, he found not one messenger as he expected, but a squad of Pinkertons. Guns blazed. Moore was wounded four times. Another bandit had his kneecap shattered. Two others, including Sparks, were wounded. All of the outlaws escaped, however, except one named Elliott. Posses raced out, and in a few hours two more wounded men, Roseberry and Clifton, were captured and taken to Cincinnati for "safekeeping."

Ten days later the three captured outlaws, guarded by Pinkertons, left the Ohio city for Brownstown, Indiana, where they were to be arraigned on charges of train robbery. Three miles outside of Seymour, the engineer saw red lights on the track. Thinking he was about to ram a freight, he braked the train to a halt. Immediately two hundred night-riders in scarlet masks surrounded the train. They were "vigilantes," men who called themselves the Scarlet Mask Society, dedicated to ridding the region of outlaws by whatever means necessary. They disarmed the badly-outnumbered Pinkerton guards and abducted the three outlaws. They were found hanging from a tree limb the next morning.

The lynchings filled Pinkerton with horror. It was the same dreadful Chartist mob in a new setting—and for a less worthy cause. Yet Pinkerton had his job to do, and he set out after Moore, Sparks and a third man, Jerrell, who were still at large. He maintained a close watch on any relatives, friends and, particularly, girl friends of the gang members. One lady friend of Jerrell's soon received a letter from Illinois. Since she couldn't read, she asked a neighbor to read it to her. A few polite inquiries and Pinkerton's men zeroed in on Moore, Sparks and the not-too-bright Jerrell, arresting them in their hideout near Mattoon, Illinois.

The outlaws were charged, jailed at Indianapolis and in a few days put aboard a train for Brownstown. They never made it. The vigilantes struck again. Three miles outside of Seymour the train was surrounded by several hundred men on horseback, wearing scarlet masks. Badly outgunned, the Pinkertons could only surrender their weapons and prisoners. At dawn, Moore, Sparks and Jerrell were hanging from the same beech tree limb that had been used to hang their comrades—a spot known today as Hangman's Junction.

There were still two elements of the Reno gang at large. Frank Reno and four other gang members had fled to Windsor, Canada. William and Simeon Reno were in hiding in Indianapolis. William and Simeon's days became numbered when Pinkerton located and arrested the pair. They were charged with train robbery and jailed at Lexington, Indiana, about forty miles south of Seymour.

Now nation-wide attention was focused on the situation. With Simeon and William behind bars, the vigilantes swore they would lynch the outlaws. At the same time, remnants of the Reno gang threatened to free them. In this situation the prisoners were moved to the sturdier jail at New Albany, eleven miles from Lexington and across the Ohio River from Louisville, Kentucky.

An uneasy quiet prevailed as the date set for the Reno brothers' trial approached—September 7. Finally, on the night of September 6, the Scarlet Mask Society struck. With military precision—they addressed each other only by number, so that none knew another's identity—they moved into Lexington and took over the main street. They herded all citizens indoors, then battered open the jail with a ram—only to find the prisoners were still in New Albany. Undaunted, the vigilantes waited for the train from New Albany and boarded it. To their disgust, the vigilantes discovered that the Renos were not on the train either.

There was a good reason why they were not on the train. Allan Pinkerton had wired New Albany from Windsor, Canada, that he had arrested Frank Reno. It was a typical example of Pinkerton's detective skill. He trailed the gang to Windsor, then watched Reno's associates until the outlaw hideout was located.

Relations between Canada and the United States were not so cordial then as now, and for two months extradition proceedings occupied the attention of high government officials in Washington, London and Ottawa. When two attempts were made to assassinate Pinkerton (both shots missed and he was able to disarm the gunmen) the United States dispatched a gunboat to Windsor to protect him. The Canadian government protested, and the Renos were page-one news in America, Canada, England and the rest of Europe.

Eventually, wearing handcuffs and leg-irons, Frank Reno and Charles Anderson, another of the gang members, were put aboard a seagoing tug which Pinkerton had ordered especially for the trip. The tug had hardly left the Windsor dock when it was rammed and cut in two by a steamer. Pinkerton, his two detectives, and the manacled prisoners were dumped into the water. But Pinkerton saved his prisoners and early in October, 1868, delivered them to the New Albany jail. Here they were put in cells beside William and Simeon Reno.

The great detective and his men had done a fantastic job, capturing the four Reno brothers and the principal members of their gang. They had followed the outlaws across several states and into Canada and delivered them safely to jail against unlikely odds. Yet the awful mob violence which had marred this case from the beginning was not yet ended. He, the nation, even the participants were only powerless spectators to the terrible events.

On December 11, 1868, a bitter cold night, members of the Scarlet Mask Society boarded a train at Seymour and in two darkened coaches started south in a locomotive without a headlight. The ghostly entourage went more than fifty miles. At Jefferson Station the vigilantes stopped to steal a second train. Other vigilantes boarded it. The two trains arrived in New Albany at 3:20 A.M.

The masked men first cut the telegraph wires. Then they stationed guards at strategic street corners, their job to keep people off the street and prevent an alarm from being sounded. The main body of the masked men headed for the New Albany jail and the sleeping Reno brothers.

The vigilantes surprised the guard who was posted outside the jail "to watch for lynchers." But he managed to scream, rather prematurely, "They've lynched the prisoners!" before being gun-butted senseless. The guard's screams awakened Sheriff Thomas J. Fullenlove. He dashed downstairs in his nightshirt, caught sight of the mob and slammed the door to his office. Moments later a ram battered it open and Fullenlove fled to the cellar, hoping to reach the rear entrance. Bullets ricocheted after him.

Fullenlove hid in the darkness of the basement a few minutes, while the men in the scarlet masks searched for him. Then, as he tried to crawl out a basement window, he was seized and pulled to his feet.

In his nightshirt, ankle deep in snow, he said: "Gentlemen, I am the sheriff—"

"Shut your dang mouth!" the number one vigilante snarled. "All we want are your keys."

"I won't give you the keys," said the sheriff, taking a step toward the masked men. "I am going to ring the fire bell. If you men have any respect for the law you will stand aside."

He started to push forward but hands grabbed him. He broke free and ran. Several shots rang out, and the courageous sheriff fell to the snow, his right arm shattered. He got up and tried to stagger for help, but the masked men caught him. Again the gun butts rose and fell in the moonlight.

Sheriff Fullenlove was dragged across the snow and into his office, where, despite the agony of his wounds, he refused to surrender the keys to the cells. He was hit in the face and still he refused. Again and again he was hit, but, moaning, he shook his head no. A masked man improved on the torture by jerking on Fullenlove's wounded arm. He shrieked in pain.

Mrs. Fullenlove rushed downstairs and tried to reach her husband. Seized by the masked men, she begged to be allowed to bandage her husband's wounds.

"Sure," number one snarled, "as soon as he tells us where the keys are."

She begged her husband to tell them, but the lawman said, "Never. I'll die first."

"All right, then we'll burn your jail with you in it."

Vigilantes frantically began breaking furniture and piling it around the helpless sheriff.

This task was interrupted by shouts from upstairs. "Here they are!" The keys had been located in Fullenlove's nightstand.

There were some further delays. A guard inside the double-tiered cellblock had to be cowed into submission, and there was some confusion about which keys matched which cell—but the tragic events moved inexorably forward.

Frank Reno was first. He kicked and fought, but the

mob seized him and dragged him from his cell. A rope was tossed over an iron beam of the roof, the noose put around Frank Reno's neck. He was shoved out into space from the second tier and died with the snapping sound of a stick being broken over a knee. William Reno, still only twenty years old, was brought from his cell, and soon his body hung next to his older brother's.

Simeon Reno fought to the last. In his frenzy he ripped a heavy iron sink from the wall and used it as a weapon, cracking the skull of one of the night-riders. Knocked unconscious by a pistol butt, Simeon Reno was bound hand and foot and hanged by the neck. Instead of being dropped so that his neck was broken, he was trussed up so he would suffocate slowly.

Then came Charles Anderson, the fourth gang member. He was tossed over the rail, but the rope broke, and he had to be pulled back up for a second, successful effort.

The vigilantes fled into the night and safety, leaving the macabre scene behind them. Simeon Reno, as his murderers figured, regained consciousness. For a half hour he thrashed, his toes just touching the floor, while prisoners in their cells screamed for help and beat their hands raw trying to get out and halt his horrible death. Sheriff Fullenlove, his wife and the guard heard, but they were bound and could do nothing to save the prisoner.

The lynchings were a sensation on both sides of the Atlantic—and one of the least savory episodes in American history. Pinkerton could think of them only with revulsion and dismay as long as he lived.

What is more amazing is that the fate of the Reno brothers did not discourage other outlaws. In the Renos' wake came Jesse James, the Youngers and many other outlaws. They created a frontier era more brutal than romantic, more sorrowful than courageous.

With the exception of the Daltons, who never robbed an express office or held up a bank protected by the Pinkerton agency, nearly every one of the outlaws was chased, captured or killed by Pinkerton's men, usually against ridiculous odds. Pinkerton tailed Jesse James, for example, for sixteen years, until the outlaw was killed by one of his own men who wanted the large reward that had been offered.

It was, truly, the Wild West, and Allan Pinkerton and his two sons, Robert and William, together with such Pinkerton men as the legendary George H. Bangs, largely maintained what law there was on the frontier, preserved some sense of order so the West could be won for ranchers, farmers and other settlers.

After his death in 1885, Allan Pinkerton's detective agency was run by his sons and then by their sons. Now well into its second century, it continues to function on the principles laid down by its founder. Pinkertons continue to protect thousands of banks, stores and factories. They were employed as official guards at the New York World's Fair. The motto of the agency is still the one coined by Allan Pinkerton: "We never sleep."

ALPHONSE
BERTILLON

Misfit with a computer mind

† The strange young man began his employment as a lowly assistant clerk in the Prefecture of Police in Paris and almost at once became something of a celebrity. Parisian officers from Prefect Louis Andrieux down to the newest detective delighted in pointing him out to visitors.

"You'll never guess who that is."

"Why no, I can't imagine," would come the incredulous reply.

"That's Alphonse Bertillon."

"You don't mean?"

"None other than his son."

When performed with appropriate gestures, at which Parisians had become most adept, the identification of Alphonse Bertillon never failed to earn a hearty laugh.

There was some humor in the situation. Alphonse Bertillon was the twenty-six-year old son of Dr. Louis Adolphe Bertillon, distinguished physician, statistician and vice president of the Anthropological Society of Paris. He was the grandson of Achille Guillard, celebrated naturalist and mathematician. Imagine! The scion of one of the most distinguished scientific families in the world working as a police clerk.

But that wasn't what people laughed at. The joke which Alphonse Bertillon provoked was a visual one, for he was a grotesque creature, pale, thin, slow, awkward, totally without grace, and afflicted with excruciating migraine headaches, remorseless indigestion and inopportune nosebleeds. If called upon to speak, he stammered for words—which came out inevitably tactless. If asked to act, he stumbled over his feet. Objects were forever dropping from his hands.

Worse, he was seemingly unfeeling about his effect on others and turned a belligerent, astringent face to the world. His temper was bad and frequently demonstrated. His attitude was sarcastic, overbearing and boorish. In short, he was a man without music in his soul. He was, in fact, so unmusical that it was said the only way he could identify a bugle call during his term in the military service was to count the notes.

Alphonse Bertillon's arrival at the Prefecture of Police in March of 1879 was the last stop on the way to oblivion. He had been expelled from the best schools in France and fired as a bank apprentice because of incompetence. He tried for a while to be a tutor in England, but cut such a ludicrous figure that he was recalled by his father, who, desperate to find some niche in life for his unfortunate offspring, used his influence to prevail upon the reluctant Prefect of Police to give him the lowest job in the department.

Low it was. Alphonse sat in a corner isolated from his colleagues. In that drizzly March he was constantly chilled. In winter his feet and hands would freeze, and in summer he would suffocate as he sat tirelessly copying on to file cards the insufferably dull data police had obtained from their arrests and interrogations. A fool could have done it—and it seemed Alphonse Bertillon was one.

Yet this strange, even bizarre individual was destined to become a remarkable detective of truly historical stature, an international celebrity—and a figure of classic tragedy.

History is made by putting the right man at the right

place at the right time—and all three came together in that dismal, drafty corner at the Prefecture of Police in 1879. Time was important because it had been seventy years since Vidocq began his police work. In that time, Vidocq's methods had been enlarged, perhaps ten thousandfold, but not really improved.

Sûreté detectives, or inspectors, as they were called, still depended on cunning and wile to trap and identify prisoners, and prided themselves on their remarkable memories. They never forgot a face. A criminal they had arrested—or even seen—years before was indelibly etched upon their matchless memories—or so they liked to believe. Standard procedure was for inspectors to visit jails and prisons once a week and view the inmates who were paraded in front of them. This supposedly added to their list of "unforgettables."

Vidocq had kept records, and in 1879 the Sûreté was still keeping records in the same old way. Information on anyone convicted, arrested or even questioned by French police was filed—but only to jog a good detective's memory, mind you. It was this information which Bertillon was transcribing to the file cards. A man's stature might be listed as "tall," "medium" or "small." Notation would be made of his eyes, facial characteristics, scars, tattoos or other marks. But with a precious few exceptions for remarkably unique-looking individuals, no mere written description of a man could enable him to be identified with absolute certainty or even, in most cases, to be picked out of a crowd.

It is true that in the 1840's the Sûreté had adopted photography. Every prisoner was photographed, and by 1879 over eighty thousand photographs had been accumulated. But these were inaccurate and frequently fuzzy. Prisoners often moved their heads or grimaced, making their photos useless for future identification.

Even if a photograph was crystal clear, how was it to be filed? Under name? Hardly. Convicts were forever changing their names. Under shape of nose? High or low forehead? Not practically. No one could figure out a classification system, and thus the Sûreté had a mountain of descriptive and photographic records which were virtually useless. There was no way to determine if an individual had been arrested before, no chance of learning whether he was wanted elsewhere—unless a detective could remember him and prove it.

By 1879 the Prefecture of Police had come to a virtual standstill in the identification of suspects. Something had to happen, or law enforcement in France—and the world over—would collapse from its own monstrous inefficiency. Clearly, some new, systematic method of identification was needed.

Enter Alphonse Bertillon. Lonely, misunderstood, humiliated, he searched for an avenue to justify his family name—and found it in those stupid cards which he incessantly filled out. Only Alphonse Bertillon could have thought of it. Only a man who had grown up in a home where anthropology was the first topic of conversation could have known that an adult can change his clothes, his hair color, even his facial expressions, but that his skeletal measurements are unchanging.

Why not identify prisoners by their measurements? It was worth a try, and Bertillon asked permission to measure convicts brought in for registration. His superiors laughed at him, but shrugged and agreed. Might as well humor the fool.

Through the hot, sultry summer of 1879 Bertillon— to the unmitigated amusement of other clerks—set to measuring convicts. With a tape he measured their height, the length and circumference of heads, length of arms, fingers, feet—and with each measurement knew he was right. In mid-August he wrote a report on his findings and sent it to Louis Andrieux. There was no reply.

Bertillon expanded his measuring activities. Before going to work in the morning, he would visit the La Sante jail and take measurements of the prisoners there. In October, shortly after being promoted from assistant clerk to clerk, he sent a second report to Andrieux. In this he pointed out that if one measurement was taken of a man, his height, for example, the chance of another man having exactly the same height was four to one. If a second measurement was added, his head circumference, say, the chances increased to 16 to 1. If eleven measurements were taken, the odds against a duplication were 4,191,304 to 1. If fourteen measurements were kept, the odds were 286,435,456 to 1. Bertillon also explained in his report his method of cataloging these measurements so that any individual file card could be found within minutes.

Two weeks elapsed while Bertillon waited nervously for a reply. Finally he was summoned before Andrieux. Stumbling over the side of his desk and brushing against the side of the door, the agitated Bertillon raced to the Prefect's office like a rampant rhinoceros.

Andrieux said he had read the report and had asked Gustave Macé, the head of the Sûreté, to read it, then unloaded his bombshell. "Bertillon, if I am not mistaken, you are a clerk of the twentieth grade and have been with us only eight months, right? Already you are getting ideas? Your report sounds like a joke."

Bertillon could only stammer, "If-if you w-will permit me-me to explain . . ."

Andrieux permitted him, but Bertillon, whose ideas were really quite simple, made them seem like a statistical bog. He was dismissed from Andrieux' presence with orders to attend to his duties—or else!

Worse, when Bertillon arrived home, his father, to whom Andrieux had complained, greeted him angrily and demanded to see a copy of the "nonsensical report." But upon reading it, the elder Bertillon was deeply moved and embraced his ugly-duckling son. "I had no longer dared to hope you would find your path in the world. This is it. This will mean a revolution in police work."

The elder Bertillon beseeched Andrieux to allow his son to continue his experiments and sent other leading Parisian scientists to badger the Prefect, but he was adamant. He would not invest an iota of time or energy in this measurements nonsense. There was nothing to do but wait until a new prefect was named.

Bertillon returned to his time-consuming, useless, ridiculous copying job, waiting for politics or time to give him his chance. It finally came in November, 1882, when Jean Camecasse, the new Prefect, gave in to the pleadings of scientists and agreed at least to consider Bertillon's method. Camecasse listened to Bertillon's involved explanation and understood not one word of it. But he was vain enough to want to be the man who had introduced a new process. So, he agreed to assign two assistant clerks to Bertillon and to give him *three months* to identify one recidivist criminal.

Bertillon felt only despair. The test was hardly fair. What was the likelihood of a man being caught, charged, sentenced, imprisoned, released and arrested again inside of three months? But it was a chance. Bertillon accepted.

The first of December, 1882, Bertillon began his test, taking measurements in the same inhospitable corner he had inhabited for three years. The clerks assigned to him were none too bright and highly unwilling. They laughed behind his back and whispered about him to the other clerks, but under Bertillon's obsessive instructions the measurements were taken.

Each night he took the cards home and transferred the measurements to file cards. Day after day it went on. By the first of the year, he had five hundred cards; by the middle of January, a thousand; by the beginning of February, sixteen hundred.

Many times Bertillon was sure he recognized one of the prisoners as having been there before. With trembling hands he checked his files—and each time he was wrong. Certainly he was proving that measurements are more accurate than memory, but that wasn't finding him a recidivist criminal.

As the days of February came and passed without success, Bertillon's desperation mounted—along with his headaches, nosebleeds and indigestion. The bad luck, abuse and despair that had plagued him all his life would not leave him now, and he cursed Camecasse for giving him only three months. *He wants me to fail, that's what he wants. He wants to have a big laugh.* Bertillon's bitterness deepened.

February 10 . . . February 15 . . . February 20— only eight more days left. . . .

Late in the afternoon of the twentieth Bertillon began measuring a man named Dupont, a name number one on the hit parade of aliases among Parisian criminals. Bertillon had already measured five other Duponts that day. It was a large ho-hum. Routinely, Bertillon began to measure this Dupont and again felt the sensation of familiarity—but dismissed the idea. He had been wrong so often.

Measurements obtained, he dipped into his files. It took only a moment—and suddenly Bertillon began to shake. "I-I've seen you before." The words would hardly come out of his excited lips. "You-you were arrested for s-stealing emp-ty b-b-b-bottles on—on December fifteenth of last year. At that t-time, you called yourself M-M-M-Martin."

Every head in the room turned to Bertillon. The smirks left every face. The policeman who had brought

Dupont in was stunned for he had failed to recognize him as an ex-convict. The electric silence was broken by Martin-Dupont who snapped, "So what if I was . . ."

Triumphant against heavy odds, Bertillon did a characteristically anti-social thing. Ignoring his co-workers, savoring none of his success, he closed up his desk and went home to tell his father. The old man died a few days later, happy that his unlikely son had found a place in life.

The day after the identification of Dupont-Martin, Prefect Camecasse extended Bertillon's experiments indefinitely. Bertillon returned to his frosty corner and continued with his measurements. In March he identified another former convict. During the following three months he found six more; in July, August and September, fifteen; and in the last three months, twenty-six—all of whom detectives had failed to spot.

As Bertillon worked, the mockery of his colleagues gave way to silence, then respect and finally admiration. Truly the man had been right. Without doubt, he was revolutionizing police methods. Imagine being able to identify a man despite aliases, despite costume changes, despite make-up and beards. Nothing a man could ever do could remove the "mark of Cain" placed upon him by nature.

What was Bertillon's reaction to the new warmth of

his colleagues? Unyielding animosity, defiance, sarcasm, coldness, distrust. He would now repay the world for mistreating him. Vengeance was to be his.

Historians say that if history is a proper amalgamation of time, place and man, the man is the least important. So it seemed to be in this instance of history, for Bertillon's system grew despite his personality, his arrogance, his pomposity, his lack of charity. By 1884 he had identified three hundred previously convicted criminals, and at the end of that year anthropometry, as he called it, or Bertillonage, as the newspapers were beginning to refer to it, was introduced into the French prison system.

In 1885 Bertillon was put in charge of a Central Office of Anthropometry to keep records and introduce his techniques into the provinces of France. Soon he was made Director of the Police Identification Service and given his own quarters, which were formally opened February 1, 1888. The next day he was saluted in the French press: "Bertillonage is the greatest and most brilliant invention the nineteenth century has produced in the field of criminology. Thanks to a French genius, errors of identification will soon cease to exist not only in France, but also in the entire world. Hence judicial errors based upon false identification will likewise disappear. Long live Bertillonage! Long live Alphonse Bertillon!" That strange duck of a man had turned into a swan.

As famous as he had become, Bertillon was never to achieve a greater triumph than in 1892, when he was brought into a crime that had shocked Europe. Since 1878 anarchism and anarchists had been the scourge of the continent. They had attempted to assassinate several reigning monarchs and, failing in that, had turned to bombings. One of several explosions which rocked a jittery Paris occurred on March 11, 1892. Dynamite went off in the dwelling occupied by Presiding Judge Benoit, who had conducted a trial of some anarchists nearly a year before.

Eventually, the Sûreté learned the bomb had been planted by an anarchist named Léon Léger, better known under another of his aliases, Ravachol. By whatever name, he was a man most wanted by police. The trouble was, hardly anyone knew what he looked like. The official description was of a man about five feet four inches tall, sallow complexion with a dark beard. In those hirsute days, that description fitted many thousands of men.

But the description, such as it was, went out through all of France and resulted in a report that a man who called himself Ravachol had lived in Saint-Étienne and

Montbrison. This provincial Ravachol's correct name was François Koenigstein. Koenigstein had a criminal record an arm long. He was suspected of smuggling and burglary, grave robbing, strangling an elderly hermit to steal his 35,000 francs, and of the hammer murder of a hardware-store proprietor—not to mention a number of other unsavory activities.

What was important was that Koenigstein, during one of his arrests, had been measured according to Bertillonage. These records were now sent to Paris and turned over to Bertillon. If Ravachol, the anarchist bomber, was ever caught and found to be Koenigstein, it would thoroughly debunk anarchism. Anarchists would be shown to be not idealistic, moralistic men who wanted to do away with all government in order to return the earth to the common man, but the commonest of criminals instead.

On March 27, 1892, there was another bombing, this time of the house of the state prosecutor. All Paris was gripped with fear, all Europe was fascinated, and the hunt for Ravachol was intensified—if that were possible. Three days after this bombing, a man fitting Ravachol's meager description was spotted in a restaurant. Five policemen arrested him, and kicking and screaming anarchist axioms, he was hauled before Bertillon. But so violent were his struggles that measuring him was impossible.

The next day the suspect had calmed down enough to be measured. He was Koenigstein all right, and eventually he admitted it.

After this *coup*, in which he identified a terrorist bomber and discredited an entire movement that was plaguing the continent, Alphonse Bertillon, still clumsy, still bad-tempered and more arrogant than ever, was the toast of Europe. The Legion of Honor was bestowed upon him. His name became a household word. Bertillonage swept into use in country after country and spread to the United States and South America.

The Frenchman, no matter how unlikable he was, had truly done a marvelous thing. He invented an improved method of criminal identification and systematized record keeping. He even cleared up the photography mess by insisting that two photographs be taken, one profile and one full face, with the camera always the same distance from the subject and with the same lighting—as it is still done today. He designed a tripod and camera for use in taking clear pictures of the scene of a crime. In short, he operated the first crime lab and introduced systematic laboratory methods into day-to-day police work.

His achievements and contributions make him, even today, a giant among detectives and criminologists.

But a man is a success only in his own eyes, regardless of what the world or history says.

Bertillon staked all his hopes on Bertillonage. It was his system, conceived, developed, perfected by him. It was to him the greatest system of identification in the world and destined to be the one system of identification.

Only it wasn't.

Even as Ravachol was being caught and identified in Bertillon's greatest triumph, Mark Twain was putting the finishing touches to his novel, *The Tragedy of Pudd'nhead Wilson*. This story, published in 1894, was plotted around a dramatic identification using a fingerprint.

Nearly forty years before, in 1857, Sir William James Herschel, British chief administrative officer in the Hooghley District of Bengal, India, had sought a system to eliminate forgeries in the payment of pensions and allowances to Indians. Since all Indians looked alike to him, he hit upon the novel idea of having the real claimant place his thumbprint on the payroll along with his "mark." When a claimant came along, he would look at the thumbprint under a magnifying glass and quickly detect an impostor. The system worked like a charm, for the superstitious Bengalese thought there was "magic" in their thumbprints.

By the 1860's Sir William had captured the interest of Sir Francis Galton, one of England's greatest scientists of the era, and of Edward Henry, a young man who had gone to India as a private secretary. Even then, enough research had been done to make it reasonably certain that each man's fingerprints were different and that they did not change in his lifetime. If marred or burned, they grew back into the same telltale ridges.

All this was known before Alphonse Bertillon developed his system of measurements. The problem was to find a way to classify fingerprints so that one man's prints could be picked out quickly from many thousands of similar prints.

A half a world away in Argentina, Juan Vucetich, a Croatian by birth and upbringing, had joined the Police Department of La Plata, Argentina, with instructions to institute the Bertillon system. He did, but he also became interested in fingerprinting. He even worked out a system of classification, and in 1892, the same year Ravachol was found by Bertillonge, Vucetich solved a murder and won a conviction on the basis of a thumbprint.

In England Sir Francis Galton worked out a system of classification in 1891, but it had some flaws. Then in 1896 Edward Henry, who had become Inspector General of Bengal police, worked out the fingerprint classification system in use today. It was adopted throughout British India in 1897 and by Scotland Yard in 1901.

At about the same time, Bertillonage suffered a severe setback as a "foolproof" means of identification. In 1903 the United States Penitentiary at Leavenworth, Kansas, found that a convict being admitted had the precise Bertillon measurements as a convict already there. Both were, in addition, named Will West and they looked remarkably alike.

The adoption of fingerprinting, meanwhile, moved forward. In 1905 a British court accepted fingerprints as evidence in a murder trial. Country after country, in Europe as well as elsewhere, began to turn from Bertillonage to fingerprinting as a means of identification. Why? If both were "foolproof," why abandon one perfectly good system just to adopt another?

The flaw in Bertillonage had been spotted by Gustave Macé, back when Bertillon first delivered his report to the disbelieving Prefect Andrieux. Macé, an old-time detective, and a good one in the Vidocq tradition, had said measurements might be all right if taken in a conscientious manner. But most police clerks were clods. Their measurements were bound to be inexact and thereby worthless.

The "cop on the beat" complained of another difficulty with Bertillonage. How did it help to identify a man on the street or at the scene of a crime? "Am I supposed to throw him down and take his measurements?" was the constant, taunting query of the practical policeman.

Bertillonage had been remarkable. As performed by the dedicated Bertillon, it *was* foolproof. It was a means of identifying and classifying prisoners and suspects badly needed at the time.

But fingerprint classification was better. Fingerprints were simple to take. The only apparatus needed was an ink pad and a piece of paper. Any cop, clod or not, could do it. And a man could be fingerprinted anywhere, not just at a police station. Finally, fingerprints were evidence left at the scene of a crime. They permitted detectives to tell not just who was who, but who did what.

To a man, the detectives of the world embraced fingerprint classification as the greatest advance in the history of law enforcement. All but Bertillon. He fought it, fingertip by fingertip. He denounced it as "tiny spots on human fingertips" and pronounced that "skin markings have insufficiently distinct gradations" to serve as identification records. He listed many "practical" objections to their use—including the fact that a prisoner's fingers became smudged!

More than picayune, more than inaccurate, he was insufferable. He slammed doors in faces of men who tried to discuss it with him. Vucetich, who tried to see the distinguished Frenchman, was greeted with an icy, "Sir, you have tried to do me a great deal of harm," whereupon Bertillon turned on his heel and stalked off. It seemed that the more Bertillonage waned, the worse Bertillon became.

Strangely, he knew of fingerprinting and, in fact, took many fingerprints, which he attached to his Bertillon file cards under "special marks." In 1902 he even solved a murder through use of fingerprints—an action which he endeavored to conceal. For him it was to be Bertillonage or nothing.

The end came in 1911, when an incredible crime occurred. The *Mona Lisa*, the greatest treasure of France, was stolen from the Louvre Museum. The French were beside themselves. The biggest police crisis in the history of the nation developed overnight.

The theft should have been solved easily, because the thief left his fingerprints on the glass case in which the Leonardo da Vinci masterpiece had hung. But try as he would, Bertillon could not identify the prints or the thief.

Twenty-eight months later, on December 2, 1913, the painting turned up in Florence, Italy, unharmed, and the thief, Vicenzo Perrugia, was arrested. It soon was learned that Perrugia had been arrested in Paris several times, the last time only two years before the theft. His fingerprints had been taken and filed—but as special marks under the Bertillon system.

If a fingerprint classification similar to that in use in most of the world had been adopted in France, Perrugia would have been identified in a few hours. As it was, the only way to have found Perrugia's prints under Bertillon's system was to go through thousands upon thousands of records—an impossible task.

Bertillon, who only a few short years before had been turned from an unlikely boor into the toast of Paris, was back where he started, an outcast, abused, denounced, ridiculed. The people of Paris clamored for his dismissal and a reorganization of the Identification Bureau. The bitterest of fates had befallen Alphonse Bertillon.

By that time his indigestion and migraines, encouraged by his fury and frustration, had worsened. Doctors diagnosed his illness as pernicious anemia—a death sentence in those days. His sight failed. He weakened rapidly, and on February 13, 1914, he mercifully died.

And with him so did Bertillonage.

Yet this strange, driven man was hardly a failure. As the father of police identification, his place among the world's great detectives was assured.

MARIE-FRANÇOIS
GORON

Bloodhound of the Sûreté

† Early in August, 1889, the residents of the village of Millery, near Lyons, France, were oppressed by an unpleasant odor. The stench seemed to emanate from the banks of the river Rhone, and with each hot August day it seemed to get worse.

Since no one else was inclined to do anything about it, the road commissioner set out to investigate. On August 13, near the river bank, he found a large burlap sack, tied at its open end. Drawing his knife, the commissioner slit open the sack—and fell backward in horror at the sight of the badly deteriorating body of a black-haired man, which fell out headfirst.

The road commissioner ran to get a policeman, and after his own investigation the policeman sent for the state prosecutor and a police physician, Dr. Paul Bernard. Since it was too dark for an autopsy, the corpse was taken to the morgue in Lyons.

The following day Dr. Bernard performed an autopsy. The body, he determined, was that of a man five feet, seven inches tall, between thirty-five and forty-five years old. Both hair and beard were black. The victim had been strangled to death, as demonstrated by damage to his larynx. After death the body had been wrapped in oilcloth, tied with twenty-five feet of string and inserted in the burlap sack.

Even as Dr. Bernard conducted the autopsy, new evidence was found. The smashed remains of a wooden trunk were discovered on the river bank. The smell of cadaver associated with the wood and the discovery of a key fitting the trunk near where the body had lain led Lyons authorities to the belief that the body had been in the trunk.

Lyons police were even able to tell where the trunk had come from. On it were two railroad labels with this information: "From: Paris 1231—Paris 7/27/188—. Express Train 3. To: Lyons-Perrache I." The trunk containing the body had been sent from Paris on Train 3 on July 27, 188—what? The last digit of the year was obscured, but considering the advanced decomposition of the body, the year must have been 1888—over a year before.

Discovery of the corpse at Millery was reported in local papers, which were in turn read at the Sûreté in Paris. The items about the corpse were red-penciled and put on the desk of the Chief of the Sûreté, and on August 17 they were read by the Chief, Marie-François Goron.

He was a remarkable detective for any age. He had been born near Rennes, France, in 1847, and served with distinction in the War of 1870. After a fling at business, he joined the Paris police in 1881. His rise thereafter was little short of fantastic. In four years he was Commissioner of Police in the Partin District of Paris. The following year he was Deputy Chief of the Sûreté and in 1887 became Paris' top detective. That also made him the world's top detective, for the Sûreté, by acclamation, was the finest detective force in the world.

In appearance Goron was short and fat, afflicted with asthma, wore a waxed mustache and pince-nez glasses— hardly the popular conception of what a detective should look like. Yet he brought to his work a number of qualities which would make a man a success in any endeavor and a particularly good detective. He was dedicated to catching criminals, approaching law enforcement with great energy and incredible thoroughness. He was a man of some education. He had read a good deal and had an artistic temperament, which he turned to the detection of crime.

One of his innovations was improved interrogation. He questioned suspects with a vengeance, keeping them hungry while tempting them with sumptuous meals, thirsty while keeping water just out of reach. He quartered them first in a dark cell and then in a brightly lit one. Worn down physically, confused mentally, they were jailed with spies and informers especially trained to pump information out of prisoners. Today this would be called the "third degree" or "brainwashing," and it worked just as well in the 1880's.

Perhaps what made Goron such a remarkable detective was his "sixth sense" about a case and his persistence in following his hunches. He was like an old bloodhound who never gives up on a scent, no matter how faint or unlikely the trail. In fact, Goron's persistence was more often obstinacy, or vanity, to prove his hunch had been correct.

On August 17, when he read the news item in the provincial papers, Goron had the strongest possible hunch that the corpse at Millery was the missing Parisian court bailiff Gouffé. More than three weeks before, on July 27, 1889, Gouffé's brother-in-law had reported his disappearance. This created no stir, for Gouffé was a grown man of forty-nine. He was entitled to go off somewhere if he wished, particularly since he was a widower and, as it developed, quite a "ladies' man." The supposition that he was off on a romantic adventure was easy to make.

When Gouffé had not returned on July 30, Goron went personally to Gouffé's office. On the floor near the safe he found eighteen burned matches. The concierge reported that on the night of the bailiff's disappearance, a man had entered the office, opened the door with a key, remained awhile, then left. She had supposed it was Gouffé, until he was leaving. Then she saw it was a stranger.

Goron then sent his men to investigate other aspects of Gouffé's life. The missing man's finances were in order, and he seemed to be in no particular trouble despite his abundance of love affairs. Literally hundreds of girls who might have known or seen the bailiff were questioned—without useful results. Finally all policemen in France were asked to locate Gouffé, who was described as slender, five feet, nine inches tall, well dressed, with a thick mane of chestnut-brown hair and a rectangular, carefully-cropped beard.

When Goron read about the corpse at Millery, he immediately telegraphed Lyons to offer his assistance in solving the crime. The authorities in the provincial city said they were quite capable of solving their own crimes —another example of the petty jealousy that has plagued police work to this day. Besides, the Lyons police wired Goron, the man in their morgue could not possibly be Gouffé. He was much younger, two inches shorter, and had black, not chestnut, hair.

Goron was not to be denied so easily. He telegraphed editors of Lyons newspapers and obtained a full account of the finding of the body at Millery. This only hardened his conviction that the dead man was the missing bailiff —a conviction that was largely without reason. There was not one shred of evidence on which to base Goron's belief. But to the rotund detective, a hunch was more than just a hunch.

On August 21 he sent a detective and Gouffé's brother-in-law to Lyons to view the body and hopefully to identify it as Gouffé. It was a most unpleasant task. The mortal remains of the Millery corpse were decomposed beyond recognition and kept in a reeking morgue with a number of bodies in little better and frequently worse condition. The brother-in-law endured, handkerchief to nose, long enough to take one quick glance, then fled. The detective stayed to attest that the hair was black and not chestnut; then he, too, headed for fresh air. That same day, the detective telegraphed Goron that the Millery corpse was definitely not Gouffé.

The Lyons police, meanwhile, began to make great strides toward solution of the hideous crime. A taxi driver, Laforge by name, volunteered the information that on July 6, 1889, he had picked up three passengers at the railroad station and helped them load a large, extremely heavy trunk into his cab. At their instructions, he had driven to the Millery area, where the trio unloaded the trunk and told him to wait. A few minutes later, the threesome returned empty-handed, and he drove them back to Lyons.

Delighted, Lyons police asked the cabby to view photographs in the "rogues' gallery," and he picked out three men who had been his passengers. By the greatest of luck, all three were in jail. On July 9, three days after their mysterious taxi journey, they had been arrested and charged with another robbery and murder.

As far as Lyons police were concerned, the case was as good as solved. Arrangements were made to inter the corpse in the cemetery at De la Guillotière.

Deep in his soul Goron felt that a mistake was being

made in Lyons, but he had neither authority nor method to prove it. Meanwhile, he had enough problems trying to find Gouffé, whose continued absence was intriguing the Paris press. Goron was beginning to come under some criticism for failure to solve the disappearance.

August passed, and no new leads were forthcoming, despite the intensive work of Goron and his men. Then, in September, they learned that on July 25 Gouffé had been seen in public with one Michel Eyraud and his girl, Gabrielle Bompard. On July 27 Eyraud and Gabrielle had vanished from Paris and had not returned. Since this was the same day Gouffé had disappeared, Goron put his men on the job of finding Eyraud and Miss Bompard, as well as the bailiff. All through October the Sûreté searched throughout France. Results: nil.

By the beginning of November, Goron was desperate enough to return to old hunches. Thus, he wrote to the Lyons police asking how the Millery case had ended. In time he received a polite letter from Lyons saying that the three convicts persisted in denying they had anything to do with the trunk or the corpse. Laforge, the taxi driver, had himself been arrested as an accessory. It was only a matter of time, however, said the Lyons police, before the suspects broke down and identified the dead man.

The Lyons official then asked a favor of Goron. The

deceased had obviously been murdered for the contents of his trunk. It had been sent over a year ago from Paris, but perhaps by chance some official at the railroad office might remember who sent the trunk. Would Monsieur Goron be so kind as to make inquiry? Sure that Monsieur Goron would cooperate, the Lyons official sent along the labels from the trunk.

Goron, who had never seen the labels, read them with the greatest excitement, for the date when the trunks had been sent, July 27, coincided with Gouffé's disappearance. It could be a coincidence—but . . .

The little detective raced to the train station and found that on July 27, 1888—the date Lyons authorities surmised the trunk had been sent—there was no record of such a shipment.

Almost unable to control himself, the volatile Frenchman asked the clerk, "What of July 27, 1889? Do you have a record for that date?"

The checking of records seemed interminable, but in the end the clerk found the following: "July 27, 1889, Train No. 3, 11:45 A.M., No. 1231. Destination: Lyons-Perrache I. One trunk, weight 105 kilograms."

So the trunk had been sent on exactly the same day Gouffé had disappeared, not to mention Eyraud and Gabrielle Bompard.

Goron knew that he had been right all along. Even if

a doctor, innumerable police, and Gouffé's own brother-in-law said the corpse at Millery could not possibly be Gouffé, he knew that it was.

On November 11 Goron rushed to Lyons to confront authorities there. The cab man was obviously lying. How could he have carried the trunk on July 8, when it hadn't left Paris until July 27? Laforge was brought from his cell and, under relentless questioning, admitted making up the entire story. He wanted to "get in good" with Lyons police.

Goron then demanded that the corpse be exhumed, and on November 12, 1889, this was done.

A master detective could have the hunch that put him on the scent of a crime. He could have the capability and persistence that brought him to the point Goron had now reached. But there was no earthly way he could prove that the nearly totally decomposed corpse was the ill-fated bailiff. It seemed that nature would now thwart Goron.

There were, however, some new kinds of experts who could identify—or at least try to identify—the corpse. Physicians who specialized in pathology were taking an interest in legal or forensic medicine. Their work in identifying bodies, in discovering the cause and time of death, and in finding other medical or physiological clues to murder was to work as big a revolution in crime and the science of crime detection as Bertillon and his measurements. It was to the credit of the remarkable French that both developments were occurring in the same country at the same time.

The exhumed corpse was taken to the University of Lyons, where the famous Dr. Alexandre Lacassagne was to perform the autopsy. Although only forty-five, he was one of the pioneers in forensic medicine, having made important studies of when death actually occurs in humans. This was a matter of no small importance, if only because many "dead men" had been buried while merely in a coma. It was the fashion of those days to rig coffins with bells so that a "corpse" could alert those above ground to his untimely awakening. Professor Lacassagne had made important contributions in methods to determine when a man was really dead.

He now tackled the problem of identifying the corpse —or rather, whether the corpse was Gouffé. A more impossible task seemed hard to imagine. After lying in the hot sun for weeks and being interred for months, the corpse had been reduced to little more than a skeleton.

By measuring the bones of the arms and legs, Professor Lacassagne concluded that the dead man was five feet, eight inches tall—and Dr. Bernard, the physician who had performed the original autopsy, admitted he had only guessed the height as five feet, seven inches.

This was an embarrassing admission for the former pupil of Professor Lacassagne. Since Gouffé's family insisted he was five-feet-nine, identification seemed to hinge on an inch one way or another.

Goron, who remained at Lacassagne's elbow during the grisly autopsy, used the newly-developed telephone to reach Paris. There, military authorities went through Gouffé's file. The Army had measured him as five feet, eight inches. With this incredible thoroughness, Goron contacted Gouffé's tailor. Yes, Gouffé had been five feet, eight inches tall.

Professor Lacassagne then found an even better clue to the dead man's identity. From malformations of the bones, he decided the victim had had tuberculosis of the right ankle and water on the knee. He must have walked with a slight limp.

Goron gave his staff in Paris no peace for days, and finally they learned that Gouffé, a most vain man, did have a slight limp, which he went to great pains to conceal. Gouffé's father remembered he had fallen as a boy and suffered with a sore ankle for a long time thereafter. Sûreté detectives even found a doctor who had treated the bailiff for water on the knee. Goron was already feeling the heady excitement of victory.

Lacassagne was to excite him still more. From examination of the teeth and other bones, the Professor decided that the dead man was older than Doctor Bernard had estimated. Lacassagne calculated that the victim was fifty years old—missing by only a year the age of the forty-nine-year-old Gouffé. Finally, Lacassagne tackled the problem of hair color, one of the major indications that the black-haired corpse could not be the chestnut-haired Gouffé.

The bailiff's hairbrush was brought from Paris and its chestnut-brown hair compared with the corpse's. But by this time simple washing of the corpse's hair had transformed it from black to chestnut. Microscopic comparison confirmed the similarity between the hairs from the brush and scalp.

Thus, on November 21 Professor Lacassagne turned to the elated Goron and said, not without a touch of the melodramatic, "I herewith present you with Monsieur Gouffé."

Certainly the long quest for law and order turned a corner that day, with the unification of the efforts of a great detective and an inspired scientist.

Goron's stubbornness in insisting on his hunch had paid off, but now he was in deeper trouble. Instead of criticism for not finding a missing bailiff, he was now under fire to solve a murder. This was a task Goron accepted with enthusiasm and energy.

First, he had a replica made of the trunk. So enamored

was Paris of the mystery that within three days twenty-five thousand people came to peer at it. This tactic paid off, for on November 26 Goron received information that the trunk must be of English manufacture.

At the same time the detective got a letter from a Frenchman living in London. He had read of the trunk in the newspapers and he had some information which might be helpful. On June 24, 1889, a Frenchwoman named Madame Vespres, who also lived in London, had referred a lodger to him. This lodger had taken a room for himself and his daughter. Four days later they had purchased a large trunk from the Zwanziger firm on Euston Road. It was this trunk which seemed similar to the one he had read about. One more item: in mid-July, the lodger and his daughter had departed with the trunk.

Goron immediately dispatched a Sûreté detective to London with photographs of the trunk. A salesman at Zwanziger's recognized the trunk and recalled that on June 11, 1889, he had sold it to a short-legged Frenchman of about fifty who was accompanied by a young lady. Anything else about him of interest? Yes, he had very large hands.

Goron decided to go to London himself. On December 19 he showed the remains of the trunk to the Zwanziger salesman, the operator of the rooming house who had written the letter, and to Madame Vespres. All three swore that was the trunk they had seen. Fine, but who was this lodger and his daughter?

Now in his element, Goron bore in with his questions. Madame Vespres said she did not believe the girl was really the man's daughter, but rather his mistress. She even knew her name: Gabrielle Bompard. The man? Well—oh, yes, Michel Eyraud.

Like a killer tiger, Goron stalked his prey, convinced he now knew who had murdered Gouffé. He had both Eyraud and Gabrielle Bompard thoroughly researched. Eyraud was an adventurer and a swindler, and though ugly and bald, quite successful with the ladies. He had put one firm into fraudulent bankruptcy and in July, 1889, had brought another firm to the verge of bankruptcy, when he disappeared. Gabrielle was the pretty runaway daughter of a well-to-do businessman. She had turned streetwalker and was considered totally corrupt and utterly without scruples.

Goron left no stone unturned until he found pictures of Eyraud. He had these copied and sent them with letters to all newspapers and to all French embassies and consulates around the world. He soon had the whole world looking for the Frenchman and the delectable Gabrielle Bompard.

On January 16, 1890, Goron received a letter postmarked from New York on January 8. The name on the envelope and the comparison of handwriting left no doubt it came from Michel Eyraud.

The suspect was most upset to read that he was wanted for questioning in the death of his dear, good friend Gouffé. He wished to be as cooperative as possible. Yes, he had fled Paris, but only to escape financial ruin brought on by the extravagance of Gabrielle Bompard. If anyone had killed Gouffé, it must have been her. "She could easily have had Gouffé murdered by one of her many lovers," Eyraud contended.

Goron received two more long letters from him on January 18 and 20. Then on the morning of January 22 Goron received the surprise of his life, as his secretary ushered an attractive young woman into his office—Gabrielle Bompard.

The detective was fascinated. His case was turning out to have all the drama he loved, and Gabrielle was a marvelous participant. As Goron later described her, "The sensuality and corruption literally oozed out of her skin."

When she entered his office, she was accompanied by an American, George Garanger, who did all the talking. While in Vancouver, Canada, on business, he had met a Frenchman named Vanaerd who was traveling with his daughter Berthe. Garanger had fallen instantly and madly in love with her. In his enamored state, he had become involved in a business arrangement with Vanaerd, who had asked him to be so kind as to return to Paris with his daughter. Garanger was only too glad to oblige, and started for Paris with the lovely Berthe.

On the voyage to Europe, Garanger discovered from reading the newspapers that Vanaerd was Eyraud and concluded that he had obviously fled with the money from their "business deal." On their trip to Paris, "Berthe" admitted she was Gabrielle Bompard and revealed her tragic life with Eyraud.

As related by Garanger, Gabrielle's was the tale of a sweet, innocent girl in love with the diabolical Eyraud. She was so in love with him that she had even made love to other men at his request. Among these was Gouffé, whom Eyraud hoped to swindle.

Garanger continued the story: on July 26 Gabrielle had invited Gouffé to her apartment on the Rue Tronson-Ducoudray in Paris. Out for the day, she had returned late in the evening to find Eyraud there, along with a red-haired stranger. Eyraud told her that Gouffé was busy elsewhere and would be unable to come. She accepted this with the love with which she accepted everything Eyraud told her. She even accepted the huge trunk from London which stood in the corner of the bedroom.

The red-haired man left a few moments later. The next morning Eyraud proposed a trip south. They went by train, taking the trunk with them. At Lyons, they rented a carriage, which Eyraud drove himself. At Millery the red-haired man turned up again and took the trunk. Eyraud then suggested a trip to America, to which she agreed. She knew nothing of murder. Anything involving Gouffé and the trunk was entirely Eyraud's doing.

Garanger finished his narrative—to which Gabrielle prettily nodded her agreement—by saying he was certain Gabrielle was innocent and had persuaded her to surrender to police as proof of her innocence.

Goron listened to the story in growing wonder—at how gullible Americans, particularly Americans in love, could be. He announced what he thought of the yarn by arresting Gabrielle on the spot. It was obvious to Goron that in America Gabrielle had realized Eyraud was finished and had decided to return with the American to blame Eyraud for everything. Eyraud, aware of her treachery, had written from New York trying to weaken her story.

If there was any man in the world capable of getting the truth out of an individual, it was Marie-François Goron, and he set to work on the sensuous Gabrielle. She was questioned day and night, kept hungry and sleepless, promised anything and everything as long as she would just tell the truth. The process continued until it must have seemed that the results of an admission of murder could be no more painful than the tortures of lying.

As well as these rather medieval techniques, Goron also remained a good detective. He had Gabrielle taken to the apartment at Rue Tronson-Ducoudray, where the landlady recognized her at once. The concierge, one of those who knew all the activities of her tenants, did not recall that Gabrielle came home late on the twenty-sixth of July. Instead, she remembered that Gabrielle had received a gentleman caller, a slender man with a dark beard and chestnut hair. Still Gabrielle lied. Later, Goron confronted her with a locksmith who remembered that on July 25 she had brought the trunk to him to have stronger iron braces put on it. Gabrielle continued to lie.

Goron persisted, with the obstinacy of which only he was capable, until, finally, early in February, Gabrielle changed her story. The new one went like this:

Eyraud decided to rob Gouffé, and she agreed to help —but only because she was in love with him. Behind the couch in her apartment was an alcove hidden by a curtain. Eyraud fastened an iron loop to the ceiling beam and drew a rope through it, then hid behind the curtain. Gouffé came to the door. Gabrielle received him in her dressing gown. They went to the couch. Gabrielle playfully placed the sash from her gown around the lovesick Gouffé's neck.

While the bailiff concentrated on Gabrielle, Eyraud sneaked from behind the curtain, tied the rope to the ends of the sash and, pulling on the other end of the rope, tried to hang Gouffé from the iron loop. But it didn't work. Gouffé screamed, and Eyraud had to choke him by hand. Then Eyraud wrapped the body in oilcloth and put it in the trunk.

Shaking with terror, Gabrielle stayed there with the trunk while Eyraud went to Gouffé's office and tried unsuccessfully to open the bailiff's safe. Next day they journeyed by train to Millery, dumped the body by the river and tossed the trunk down an embankment, watching it smash to bits.

Goron accompanied Gabrielle to the murder apartment and there found the iron loop and parts of the rope used in the attempt to hang Gouffé. Then the detective accepted her confession, although he personally believed she was not an ingenue forced into an accomplice role, but a willing participant.

Gabrielle's confession was the sensation of Paris. Thousands turned out to view the murder apartment, and when Gabrielle was taken to Lyons to retrace the steps of the crime, cavalry had to be called out to restrain the crowd.

But where was Eyraud? Once again Goron sent warrants to all French embassies abroad, and Eyraud was soon found. A Frenchman living in Havana, Cuba, recognized him on May 19, and he was arrested. On May 24 two Sûreté inspectors left by ship to bring him back. When the vessel returning the murder suspect docked in Saint-Nazaire on June 30, a huge crowd was present.

The trial of Eyraud and Gabrielle began December 16, 1890. Gabrielle's defense was that she had been hypnotized as a child and all her acts since then had been the result of post-hypnotic suggestion. There was much testimony about hypnosis, a new and intriguing subject in those days. On December 20 Eyraud was sentenced to death, Gabrielle to twenty years in prison.

In his remaining years with the Sûreté, Goron solved many other cases. But none was quite so famous as this one, in which a detective's logic and persistence, together with scientific acumen, solved a bizarre crime.

In retirement, the great detective wrote his memoirs. He died in 1933 at the age of eighty-six.

JOHN
WILSON
MURRAY

The player of hunches

† The corpse was found on a cold, windy February day in the dead of a Canadian winter. Two woodsmen, crossing the desolate Blenheim Swamp in southeastern Ontario, found the body of a man—or was it a boy?—crumpled in the snow, two bullet holes in the back of his head. There was no identification.

Since it occurred in the province of Ontario in the year 1890, the murder automatically brought onto the scene one of the great detectives of all time, John Wilson "Old Never-Let-Go" Murray. A fantastic individual he was, and an incredible detective.

He was born in Edinburgh, Scotland, in 1840, the scion of a seafaring family. Both his father and his grandfather had been sea captains. Unfortunately, his mother died when he was quite young, and he was reared by an aunt when his father went to sea. At age five he was taken to New York to live, only to be brought back to Edinburgh a half dozen years later.

Far from happy with his life, young Murray ran away from home when he was thirteen, and shipped aboard a coastal vessel bound for Liverpool. There his father found him and took him to Washington, D. C. He ran away again, sailing to the West Indies and back. Next he shipped aboard a vessel in the Great Lakes. All this was postponing the inevitable, and Murray was sent home by the shipowners and returned to school in 1856.

The following year there was no holding Murray, and he enlisted in the United States Navy, serving on the battleship USS *Michigan*, which plied the Great Lakes. He remained on the vessel throughout the Civil War.

When the war ended, he joined the U. S. Secret Service, which Pinkerton had established, then in 1868 entered the police department of Erie, Pennsylvania, as a detective. His abilities attracted the attention of the Canadian Southern Railway and he was invited to head the line's force of detectives. Two years later he was named detective for the Department of Justice of the government of the Province of Ontario, eventually earning the title of Chief Inspector of Criminal Investigation for the Ontario government.

By age thirty-five Murray had complete charge of criminal investigations in a huge area ringed by Quebec on the east, Manitoba on the west, the U.S. on the south and the Georgian Bay on the north, an often desolate, sometimes brutal precinct of 101,733 square miles. Yet his work often took him over a far larger territory.

Perhaps his most notable travels occurred after a forger named Davidson was arrested in Mexico and turned over to him. Under the laws of the time, the moment the prisoner was taken on any other than British territory, he could demand and receive his release. Murray's only way out was to take him aboard a British flagship traveling to a British port. Thus, he took him to Jamaica. Since no British ship to Canada was available, he sailed with him to South America, then back to the West Indies and finally to England before finding a ship that could transport the prisoner and himself to Canada. The voyages took over four months and covered twenty thousand miles—which is one of the reasons Murray was called "Old Never-Let-Go."

Murray's perseverance and several other qualities that made him a great detective were to be tested in the Blenheim Swamp murder, generally considered his finest case.

Not the least obstacle was the weather and the terrain. The cold Canadian winter, the tangled wilderness of the swamp made a forbidding setting. Worse, there seemed to be no clues with which a detective could work.

Murray studied the victim. He was a young man, hardly more than a boy. The tenderness of his hands, the seeming innocence of the face indicated to Murray that the lad came from a good class of society. He had led too sheltered a life to end up in a place like this, Murray felt. But who was he? The suit he wore had an English cut, and his undergarments were made only in England. Did this mean the young man was English? Murray guessed that it did, but he knew it was only a guess.

Certain it was that the murderer didn't want his victim identified. All the tailoring marks had been cut from his suit. The label had been ripped from his bowler hat. Even the buttons had been removed. Murray went over the body and the clothing carefully and shook his head. There was nothing to help in an identification. He would have to trust to luck to bring some help. He had the body photographed and the picture, together with a description, sent all over the world.

Murray returned to the spot where the body was found and made a thorough search for clues. All day he tramped the area, cold and wet and weary—and found nothing. He returned a second time and went over the ground on his hands and knees. Water and mud reached past his elbows and froze. Brambles tore at his face and clothing—and it was all an immense waste of time.

"Old Never-Let-Go" then lived up to his nickname. He returned to the swamp once more and again searched on all fours. Late in the afternoon, when even he was about ready to admit there must not be anything to find, Murray found something—a cigar holder with an amber mouthpiece bearing the initials "F.W.B."

Now Murray began questioning people living in and near the swamp, hoping for eyewitnesses to the murder. But this work was soon interrupted. A Reginald Birchall and his wife had asked to see the body. They had seen the photograph in the newspaper and believed they could identify the victim.

The detective ushered them into the morgue. The sheet was pulled back and Birchall and his wife glanced at the body. Mrs. Birchall gasped and looked away, while Birchall shook his head sorrowfully. "I'm afraid we know him all right," said Birchall softly. "It's poor Benwell. How did this ever happen to him?"

Murray escorted the couple to a nearby office, where he asked Birchall to tell him what he knew of the young man.

"Not much, really," said Birchall. "His name was Francis W. Benwell and he came from England. Mrs

Birchall and I made his acquaintance on our last Atlantic crossing. He was a friendly chap, and we enjoyed his company during the voyage. On reaching America we traveled as far as Niagara Falls together, and there Benwell left to continue his journey to London, Ontario. That was the last I saw of him—until just now, poor devil. I wonder who could have done this awful thing to him?"

Murray continued writing in his notebook. "I'm sure we'll find out in due time, Mr. Birchall." He made a few more notes. "Have you any idea what his business was in Canada?"

Birchall hesitated and frowned. "No—no, I don't think I know."

"Was he visiting someone perhaps? A relative? Friend?"

Birchall's frown deepened, and he looked to his wife for help. But she only shook her head that she had no information. "I'm sorry, Inspector. You know how much I want to help—but if he said anything about his plans, I'm afraid neither my wife nor I recall it."

"Try to remember. It would be most helpful."

Murray watched the furrowed expression on Birchall's face as he tried to size up this fellow. He was a man about thirty with brown eyes and a small moustache. His clothes were in perfect taste. His manners were polished and his speech precise. There was a grace to him which gave him the unmistakable look of a gentleman. He was slender, athletic, well built—perhaps five feet, nine inches, Murray estimated. All in all he struck Murray as a man of the world, accustomed to living well and enjoying life. He appeared most likable and attractive.

The detective studied the woman a moment. She was slender, blonde, pretty without being beautiful, and obviously a woman of refinement.

There was nothing in the manner of either to suggest they were anything other than they appeared to be, and yet—

"I'm truly sorry, Inspector. We both truly want to do everything we can to help bring this heinous murderer to justice, but we've told you all we know."

"I'm sure you have, Mr. Birchall. But perhaps in Niagara Falls, where you last saw young Benwell, we could discover some evidence of the—"

"A capital idea, Inspector. We were just going back there. Why don't you come with us and together we might . . ."

The words sort of dribbled to a stop for Murray was already shaking his head no. "I can't. I have pressing duties here. But I'll be finished in a few days. Why don't I meet you in Niagara Falls on—oh, say Sunday."

Birchall agreed, and the couple departed.

Murray pondered his two informants for quite some time. Their story made sense. They appeared to be people of quality, quite unlikely to be mixed up in a sordid affair of this nature. Yet, Murray couldn't get it out of his head that Birchall was lying, cleverly, expertly, yet lying—and in depth. Somehow both he and his story were fabrications.

The detective tried to discount his own hunch. He had not one fact on which to base his feeling. Surely a man who had gone to elaborate pains to make a body unidentifiable would not then turn up to make the identification. And Murray was sure the identification was correct. His cigar holder with the F.W.B. initials indicated Birchall had told the truth.

Yet Murray felt a detective was only as good as his ability to judge character, and his judgment told him this couple was phony. He needed time to check them out. His first step was to wire the police at Niagara Falls, Canada, giving the description of Birchall and his wife, along with these instructions: Shadow this man. Do not arrest him unless he tries to cross the river to the States. I will be there Sunday night." It was a tremendous risk to authorize the arrest of an apparently respectable man, but he had to keep him in Canada. He couldn't let them escape.

Immediately, Murray went to London, Ontario. Here he began to make inquiries. It was soon apparent that Francis W. Benwell had never set foot in the town, nor had anyone there ever heard of him. Birchall was lying in at least one respect. But what did that prove?

Murray next went to Niagara Falls and took the biggest risk of his life. He had Birchall and his wife arrested and charged with the Blenheim Swamp murder. It was a step quite beyond reason. He had no evidence beyond pure hunch and simple inspiration. If he were wrong, this couple could bring charges against him. His career as a police detective would end abruptly and in disgrace. Murray gulped and deep in his soul shuddered a little, for he knew he not only had to be right about Birchall— he had to prove it in a court of law.

The detective worked day and night, investigating Birchall's activities in Niagara Falls. He soon came upon a young man named Pelly who was staying at the same hotel as the Birchalls. Pelly, like Benwell, was a young Englishman of sensitivity and good family. Pelly was the son of a clergyman, a young man obviously well reared. His story was that he had read an advertisement in a London newspaper. He even had a copy of it:

> *Canada*—University man having farm wishes to meet gentleman's son to live with him and to learn the busi-

ness with a view to partnership; must invest five hundred pounds to extend stock; board, lodging and five
per cent interest till partnership arranged.

Pelly said he had found the ad most intriguing and
had arranged to meet the man who had placed it—
Birchall. Pelly said he had listened to such glowing accounts of life in Canada, the lush farmlands and the
great opportunity for one to make his fortune that he
could not resist. He just had to go, and since he lacked
the necessary 500 pounds, he was allowed to pay only
170 pounds.

As he was preparing to leave for Canada with the
Birchalls, the party was joined by Benwell, who was also
answering the ad. Pelly admitted he thought it peculiar
that Birchall had taken in more than one partner, then
dismissed the suspicion when he learned that Benwell
also had been short the 500 pounds. It was reasonable
that Birchall should have to take in additional partners
to raise the capital.

The voyage to the new world was agreeable and
the foursome traveled pleasantly to Buffalo, where all
checked into the same hotel.

"After we had been there a few days," Pelly said,
"Birchall and Benwell went off to Canada to see the
farm in which they had invested."

"Then what happened?" asked Murray.

"Why, nothing—except that Birchall came back alone."

"You didn't think that strange?"

"Well—no. Birchall seemed in such excellent spirits when he returned that day. I asked about Benwell, of course—but he explained that Benwell had not liked the farm and had remained in Canada to visit some people to whom he, Birchall, had introduced him. It made sense and I thought little of it—until . . ."

"Until what?"

"I saw a picture in the paper. I knew it was Benwell and I insisted that Birchall return to Canada to identify the poor devil."

Murray was elated. At last he had an explanation why Birchall had identified the body he had earlier sought to make unidentifiable. But he was far from having a court case. "Do you remember the date Benwell and Birchall went to Ontario?"

He gave a date in February which coincided with the one Murray figured to be the murder date.

The detective asked Pelly if there were any circumstances that had made him suspicious of Birchall. Indeed there were! Pelly had gone with Birchall to visit the Niagara Falls, and together they had taken some secluded steps down near the river. A stranger was there, and looking back on it, Pelly figured the man's presence had saved his life. The next day Birchall had invited him to stand near the edge of the Falls, but some instinct had kept Pelly from advancing any closer.

"There was a third incident," Pelly said, his face blanching from fear just remembering it. "We walked over to the United States side of the river and then came back over the lower suspension bridge. It was storming and blowing when, near the center of the bridge, Birchall walked to the edge and looked down on the roaring rapids. 'Come see the view,' he said. 'It's superb.' I drew back. I knew better than to go there. Birchall grew white and walked on. I lagged behind out of his reach. 'Come walk with me,' he said, beckoning to me. I shook my head. He urged me to come beside him, but I continued to refuse. He started toward me and I stepped back. I was just about to run across the bridge when two men came walking over the bridge. I'm sure they saved my life."

Murray was now increasingly certain that his hunch about Birchall had been right, and he sought new evidence. From Scotland Yard he learned that Birchall had been a student at Oxford University, but had to leave after some sort of trouble. Then he had eloped with the daughter of a railway official. Scotland Yard reported that Birchall seemed to have no source of income, yet he had money. He and his wife lived by their wits, some-

times calling themselves "Lord and Lady Somerset."
They were suspected of having swindled many people.

Grimly, Murray pursued the case, seeking to trace
Birchall's movements on the day of the murder. Traveling the same train he and Benwell had taken and questioning the crews and station employees, Murray traced
the murderer and his victim to Eastwood, four miles
from Blenheim Swamp.

Still unsatisfied, Murray set out to question anyone
who had been within miles of the murder scene and,
after many hours of fruitless work, found a girl who had
actually seen Birchall and Benwell together near the
swamp. He found a timber cutter who had heard the
shots from a mile away.

In growing elation Murray kept at it, prowling around
Eastwood, questioning local people. Finally he located
a farmer who could identify Birchall as the man he had
seen coming from the swamp an hour after the shots
were heard—alone. Finally, the detective found a girl
who had actually known Birchall as "Lord Somerset"
and had seen him at Eastwood Station.

A final piece of evidence came from England. Three
days after the crime, Birchall had written to Benwell's
father in England, dunning him for the 100 pounds his
son still owed on the 500-pound "debt."

Mrs. Birchall was released, but Birchall was tried,

convicted and hung. Through bold action and tireless work, "Old Never-Let-Go" Murray had turned the flimsiest of suspicions into one of the world's masterpieces of detection.

SIR BERNARD
SPILSBURY

 |||||

Genius with a microscope

† As a murder mystery it read like fiction and, in fact, hundreds, perhaps thousands of stories, novels, movies and television plots have been based upon the murder of Mrs. Cora Crippen. Chances are, however, that none of the stories quite matches the drama of the real case.

The year was 1910 and although the world hardly knew it then, a centuries-old order was drawing to a close. The age of monarchies, chivalry and the good, peaceful life would soon end in the mud and blood of World War I, to be replaced by the violence and uncertainty the world has known ever since. The elegance of the old era would give way to fantastic technological advances, its courtly manners to the haste and rudeness of expediency.

In 1910 the forces of both the old and the new eras were vying with each other, and in the field of crime the Crippen murder was a reflection of both forces. The murder was a sensation on both sides of the Atlantic, enthralling millions of people, for it combined love, macabre violence, and a matchless chase with new technology and science. The Crippen murder also saw the rise of a great new scientific detective.

On June 30, 1910, Chief Inspector Walter Dew of Scotland Yard's Central Intelligence Division, which was already replacing the Sûreté as the world's best detective force, was summoned into the office of his superior, Superintendent Frank Froest. There Dew met Mr. and Mrs. Nash, who had come to ask the Yard to investigate a missing person, a Mrs. Cora Crippen.

Mrs. Nash, who did most of the talking, explained that she was a stage performer under the name of Lil Hawthorne and was a member of the Music Hall Ladies' Guild. Mrs. Crippen, who had performed under the names of Cora Turner and Belle Elmore, was likewise a Guild member. Mrs. Nash said that Mrs. Crippen had last been seen on February 1. The nature of her disappearance was such that it had led Mrs. Nash to make her own investigation.

On January 31 last—Mrs. Nash fetched a piece of paper from her cavernous purse and glanced at some notes she had scribbled on it—Mr. and Mrs. Paul Martinetti had been guests in the home of Dr. and Mrs. Crippen. It had been a rather ordinary evening, although Mrs. Crippen and her husband had quarreled a little. This was not uncommon, for the two were often rather tense in their relationship.

On February 3, the notes revealed, the Music Hall Ladies' Guild had received two letters from Mrs. Crippen saying that she had to leave immediately for California to attend a relative who was seriously ill there. But, Mrs. Nash said, the letters were not in Mrs. Crippen's handwriting! She, herself, had asked Dr. Crippen about his wife and so had Mrs. Martinetti and several other ladies of the Guild, and Dr. Crippen had been most uncommunicative.

What really alarmed Mrs. Nash, a woman of considerable propriety, was that entirely too soon after Mrs. Crippen left for California, Dr. Crippen began to be seen in public with his secretary, Ethel Le Neve. They even went to a dance together, and the girl was even seen to wear Mrs. Crippen's furs and jewelry—if one could imagine such a thing!

Then—Mrs. Nash referred to her paper again—on March 12, Miss Le Neve had moved into Dr. Crippen's home. A dozen days later he had sent out black-bordered announcements that Mrs. Crippen had died of pneumonia in California. Since Mrs. Crippen was only thirty-five and known to be in excellent health, this story seemed less than reliable to Mrs. Nash. She asked if Scotland Yard would investigate to determine what had really happened to Cora Crippen.

This was a routine inquiry. In a city the size of London and in a country as cosmopolitan and powerful as Great Britain in 1910, individuals were constantly on the move. For Mrs. Crippen to leave her husband and for him to move his secretary into his home in her absence might make good gossip, but it was hardly surprising in the twentieth century.

What was surprising was that Inspector Dew investigated this rather unlikely matter. He could easily have assigned it to one of the men under him, but he took the time and trouble to look into it himself, probably because Superintendent Froest was interested.

Inspector Dew was an excellent example of why Scotland Yard was so good. He was a country boy, one of eleven children, whose father had migrated to London with the family when Walter was ten. He had little schooling, having left when he was thirteen. He had worked as a clerk and as a railroad guard and then joined the Metropolitan Police (Scotland Yard) when he was nineteen. Now as a high-ranking detective, he was all the Yard liked its men to be, intelligent, resourceful, patient to a virtue and stubborn to a fault. There was nothing flamboyant about Dew. He didn't appear brilliant. Plodding was the way most people thought of him and other Scotland Yard detectives, careful, incredibly thorough and grimly determined.

Dew began by making inquiries about Mrs. Crippen, and he learned that the story related by Mrs. Nash was substantiated by other friends of the missing woman. Having gotten nowhere, Dew and another detective went on July 8, 1890, to the Crippen house at 39 Hilldrop Crescent. It was, as Dew described it, "a large, semi-detached dwelling of the old type, well back from the road and partially screened by overgrown trees."

Dew's knock was answered by a French maid who, apparently having difficulty conversing in English, motioned them to a bright, comfortable parlor decorated in the fashion of the day. A few minutes later a young woman appeared. Dew surmised this was Ethel Le Neve. She was a slender girl, "not pretty," as Dew put it, "but attractive and neatly and quietly dressed."

Politely—Scotland Yard men are always polite—Dew introduced himself and the other detective and said he wished to speak to Dr. Crippen. Then added, "We have been asked to make some inquiries about Mrs. Crippen."

The girl did not blush or seem disturbed. "I'm afraid Dr. Crippen is not here now," she said. "He's at his office in Albion House on New Oxford Street."

Dew hesitated, then asked, "You are Ethel Le Neve, I presume."

Now the girl blushed slightly. "Yes, I am."

"I thought as much. Would it impose on you too much to accompany us to Albion House?"

"Why no. I'll get my things."

Dew's point in asking Miss Le Neve to accompany them to Crippen's office was simply to prevent her from warning him they were coming. However, when they reached the entrance to Albion House, Miss Le Neve said there was no need for them to climb to the third floor, where the doctor's offices were. She would ask him to come down, and she was off before Dew could stop her.

Dew was only halfway up when Crippen came down to meet them. He was a man about fifty, small in stature, with a large moustache and enormous, protuberant eyes. With Dew he was quite calm and most polite.

The detective spoke first. "I have come to ask if you can offer an explanation as to your wife's disappearance."

Crippen sighed. "I suppose," he said, "I had better tell the truth."

"Yes," said Dew, "that would be better."

Crippen's sigh deepened. "The stories I have told about my wife's death are untrue. As far as I know she is still alive."

With that surprising statement, Crippen invited the detectives to his office and for the next five hours told a most effective story. His manner was that of a much-maligned man eager to clear up the matter with the truth.

He was born in Cold Water, Michigan, U. S. A., in 1862, and after attending the University of Michigan, had received his M.D. at Hospital College in Cleveland. He had interned at the Ophthalmic Hospital in New York, where he had begun to specialize in eye, ear, nose and throat maladies. In 1892 he had met a seventeen-year-old beauty who called herself Cora Turner or Belle Elmore. She was, when he met her, a patient of a colleague of his.

Crippen fell hopelessly in love with Cora and married her. Only then did he learn her real name was Kunigunde Mackamotzki, whose father was a Russian Pole and mother German. She was avaricious by nature and most ambitious. She wanted to be a star of the musical stage, but possessed only a diminutive singing voice.

Crippen paid for innumerable singing lessons, which did little but decrease his fortune and heighten his distaste for music.

In 1900, at her suggestion, they moved to London, where Cora hoped her theatrical abilities would be more in demand. Alas, she was able to get only two singing engagements. Cora vigorously blamed Crippen for her failure and, since she was a domineering woman, kept pushing him to make more money. This was difficult. Since he was not licensed to practice medicine in England, he was reduced to selling patent remedies. Cora also sought to improve her social position by entertaining lavishly. On these occasions she treated Crippen more like a lackey than a husband, forcing him to run errands and serve guests.

Finally, Crippen said, his wife had met an American named Miller, who was far more affluent than he, and had run off with him. Crippen said he had invented the tale of her death to avoid the scandal and the many explanations to their friends.

Crippen frankly admitted his relationship with Miss Le Neve. They had fallen in love, and Mrs. Crippen had found it out. That might have been one of the reasons she had gone off with the rich American. The physician said he and Miss Le Neve had continued to see each other after Mrs. Crippen left, and finally the secretary had come to live in his home as his wife, even to the extent of wearing Mrs. Crippen's jewels and furs. Crippen said he was not going to maintain that his conduct was proper, yet he felt he was entitled to some happiness in his lifetime.

As Dew listened and made notes on Crippen's story, he had to admit it was most orderly and quite convincing. It also was proof that Crippen was a most accomplished liar—if not now, certainly in his earlier tale to Cora's friends.

Dew then said, "I have to find Mrs. Crippen to clear up the matter."

The doctor agreed and offered to do everything he could to help. Dew suggested that perhaps if he searched the house, he might find some evidence of where she had gone. Crippen nodded and with Ethel Le Neve accompanied the detective to the house on Hilldrop Crescent.

Dew went through the house carefully, examining all drawers and cupboards, while Crippen and Miss Le Neve hovered nearby answering questions and making suggestions. Dew even went into the coal cellar, a damp place without lights. The detective formed the impression that Cora Crippen had an extraordinary assortment of clothing, including "enough ostrich feathers to start a millinery shop."

The only out-of-the-way item Dew discovered was a gun. When he emerged from the cellar, the detective happened to glance a second time in a drawer and spotted the weapon. Since it had not been there the first time, Dew could only conclude that Crippen had been carrying it during the search.

Dew's suspicions were not particularly aroused by any events of the day. Crippen's story was plausible and neither he nor Miss Le Neve acted the part of murderers. Considering the obviously greedy nature of Cora Crippen, it was easy to assume she might have run off with a richer man.

Two days later, on Monday, Dew returned to Crippen's office in Albion House to ask additional questions —and discovered the doctor and Ethel Le Neve had fled. Questioning a handyman, Dew learned that Crippen had gone to his office on Saturday morning, the day after Dew's visit, and sent the handyman to the store to buy some *boys'* clothing, including a brown tweed suit, brown felt hat, two shirts, two collars and a pair of boots, tan in color.

Where Dew had not been suspicious before, he now most certainly was. But suspicion was all he had. There was not a single shred of evidence on which to seek a warrant for the arrest of Crippen and Ethel Le Neve. Dew felt the answer to this puzzle lay in the house on

Hilldrop Crescent, so he again searched the house from attic to cellar. He searched it all day and half the night—and found nothing. He returned the next day and again searched in vain.

By the third day, Dew was bone weary and frustrated at his failure to find any evidence that Crippen and his girl friend had done other than go off on a holiday. But in the finest traditions of English detectives—it is his persistence which makes the British detective feared the world over—Dew said to his sergeant, "We might as well have another go at that coal cellar."

They had already had several "goes" at the cellar, but they started in again, with Dew on his hands and knees poking at bricks in the floor. After a protracted interval, he found a loose brick. It was pried out, followed by others, until a patch of earth was laid bare. A shovel was brought in and the earth scraped away—to reveal one of the grislier sights in the history of murders.

The following day, July 14, Dr. Augustus J. Pepper, surgeon and government pathologist, viewed the remains in the coal cellar and supervised the removal to the Islington morgue. What he had was a human body which someone with an excellent command of anatomy had set out to make unidentifiable. The corpse was headless and limbless, its bones removed to prevent identification.

The coal cellar was mined for all it was worth. Portions of a pair of ladies' pajamas were found, and Cora's friends said that she had indeed owned a pair just like them. Interesting, but hardly proof the individual in the cellar was Cora Crippen—or even a woman at all.

Pepper began his autopsy and turned over the recognizable internal organs to Dr. William Willcox, another pathologist, for analysis for poison. Then Pepper's examination turned up an interesting find, a patch of wrinkled skin measuring 5½ by 7 inches. The pathologist knew wrinkling occurs after death and such could be the case here. But, as a surgeon, he felt the welts on this skin resembled a surgical scar. This hunch was substantiated when Dew learned from friends of the late Mrs. Crippen that she had undergone major abdominal surgery in New York.

The job of proving that this was indeed a surgical scar from the abdominal area fell to a thirty-three-year-old pathologist, Dr. Bernard Spilsbury. Tall, slim, handsome, elegant, never seen without a flower in his buttonhole, he was a far cry from the public image of the habitué of morgues. In fact, he had not started out to be a pathologist. Though his father was a chemist, Spilsbury had no particular interest in science. More by chance than by design, he became a medical student, but in school, while bent over microscopes, he found his life's passion—forensic pathology.

Practically living in morgues and laboratories, he became an acknowledged expert in tissue changes. Endowed with thoroughness and highly trained powers of observation, he could detect with the naked eye changes death makes in human tissue that others failed to see with a microscope. Since he had made a special study of scar tissue, it was only natural that he be called in to study the skin from the corpse in the coal cellar of the house on Hilldrop Crescent.

Dew, meanwhile, was far from idle. A detailed description of Crippen and Ethel Le Neve was sent out, and in five days Dew got the answer to a detective's prayer. He received a telegram from the captain of the SS *Montrose* which was at sea bound for Quebec from Antwerp, Belgium. The captain said he had boarded passengers in Brussels who identified themselves as John Robinson and son. Much about this pair made him suspicious. The "boy" looked quite effeminate. "He" was constantly wearing his hat, and his clothes were the worst possible fit. On one occasion he had seen the "son" squeeze the father's hand, which hardly seemed the proper father-son relationship. The captain had even spoken to Mr. Robinson by name, but he had not answered. All this led the captain to suspect the Robinsons were Crippen and Ethel Le Neve.

Dew thought so, too, and boarded the fast liner *Laurentic* in an attempt to outrace the *Montrose* across the Atlantic. The whole world watched the race, and a great throng was on hand when Dew arrived at Quebec— ahead of the *Montrose*. For the next several hours Dew was busy fending off American and Canadian reporters who were floating a raft, determined to get on board the inbound *Montrose* as "shipwrecked sailors" and thus get the story of Crippen and his "boy bride." Dew was hard-pressed to forestall these journalistic adventures and keep control of his investigation—a problem every detective would have in the years to come.

Secretly, Dew went out by launch to meet the *Montrose*. On board he walked up to the unsuspecting Robinson and, despite the beard which the doctor had grown, recognized the protruding eyes. "Good morning, Dr. Crippen," he said, and the physician surrendered meekly. Ethel Le Neve was arrested in her cabin, obviously relieved to be able at last to end her masquerade as a boy. The couple was returned by ship to England to be greeted on August 10 by an immense crush of people at the dock.

Through all these harrowing weeks, Crippen bore up well—and won many admirers. His concern for Miss

Le Neve was most touching. He tried in every possible way to relieve her of any involvement in the crime and to spare her as much suffering as possible. All this was detailed in syrupy reports in papers around the world, for the illicit romance, the brutal nature of the murder, the first use of transatlantic telegraph to catch a criminal, and the boat race all made the Crippen case a sensation.

The continent-hopping work of Dew and Scotland Yard made the headlines, but the issue of innocence or guilt was still to be decided by work being done by Bernard Spilsbury. Unless he could prove that the small piece of wrinkled skin was an abdominal scar, the state's case against Crippen and Miss Le Neve would collapse. No one could prove that the corpse in the coal cellar was Cora Crippen or that her husband had murdered her.

On August 20, ten days after the suspect was returned to England, Scotland Yard got its first break. In a marvelous piece of lab work, Dr. Willcox, the pathologist, succeeded in identifying the poison used to kill the body in the cellar. By new and startling methods, he revealed that the vegetable poison hyoscine had been the fatal potion. This was a valuable clue, for in a few days of hard digging, Dew found that five grains of hyoscine had been delivered to Dr. Crippen's office and that he had never been known to use this compound previously.

The case against Crippen was building. On September 15, after eight weeks of work, Spilsbury completed his analysis. Exhaustive study of the skin, its hairs, its muscular structure, the peculiar formation of its cells all showed—under microscopic analysis—that this was indeed an abdominal scar.

The trial of Crippen and his girl friend began on October 18, 1910, and a hard-fought one it was. Crippen's skillful attorney sought to prove the woman's body had been buried in the cellar prior to Crippen's moving into the house. The testimony of Spilsbury was cleverly attacked. After all, he was only thirty-three, new in his work, and hardly an authority.

Crippen's lawyer had not counted on the courtroom presence of Spilsbury. The handsome pathologist was a most impressive witness. He carefully explained his findings to the jury. A microscope was mounted, and each member of the jury looked at the specimens Spilsbury had prepared, while he told them exactly what they were seeing.

On October 22, after deliberating only twenty-seven minutes, the jury found Crippen guilty, Miss Le Neve innocent. He was hanged four weeks later.

The Crippen case made Bernard Spilsbury famous. British juries, which had previously been suspicious of forensic medicine, now began to give great weight to the findings of an autopsy or other pathological study. And if Spilsbury was the expert witness, the result was almost certain conviction.

His reputation as an expert medical witness was world-wide. Every mortuary in the United Kingdom installed a special table for Dr. Spilsbury. In 1922 he was knighted by King George V.

For over three decades Spilsbury dominated forensic medicine in England. A strange, intense man, he worked almost all the time. It was estimated he performed twenty-five thousand autopsies in his lifetime, and although he worked with great speed, he was able to accomplish his tasks only at the sacrifice of family and other pleasures most men take for granted.

Seemingly driven to learn as much as he could about the causes of death, Spilsbury took on much extra work he didn't have to do, including helping coroners and advising detectives on their cases.

Eventually, he began to make some mistakes. One occurred in 1925, in the trial of Norman Thorne, charged with the murder of his girl friend, Elsie Cameron.

Elsie's headless, limbless remains were found buried on a poultry farm operated by Thorne. He admitted he had cut up Elsie's body and buried it—but he had not killed her. His story was that Elsie, during a visit to his farm, had demanded that he marry her. He refused and stalked out of the house. On his return, he found her hanging from a rafter. Afraid of being blamed for her death, he buried the body.

Spilsbury examined the remains. He studied the neck region and could find no evidence of hanging—but he did not prepare tissues for microscopic examination. He simply announced the girl was badly bruised and had been beaten to death.

Thorne's attorneys recruited a battery of forensic pathologists who examined the neck tissue microscopically and concluded that Elsie had been hanged. She was not dead when Thorne cut her down, however, and in dragging away the unconscious body, the suspect had inflicted the bruises that Spilsbury considered a beating.

The experts confronted each other at Thorne's trial. Spilsbury insisted the testimony of the defense experts was incorrect. The issue came down to which experts were to be believed.

The jury believed Spilsbury. Juries habitually did. In fact, the judge had explained to the jury that Spilsbury's opinion was without doubt the best that could be obtained. Verdict: guilty.

Before the trial ended, however, Thorne's lawyer cried out, "We can all admire attainment, take off our hats to ability, acknowledge the high position that a man has won in his sphere. But it is a long way to go if you have to say that when a man says something, there can be no room for error."

And clearly Spilsbury had erred in not making the microscopic analysis.

There were other cases in succeeding years in which Spilsbury won a verdict but damaged his reputation among his colleagues in forensic medicine. This tended to make him more stubborn and less willing even to consider the possibility that he could be wrong.

While not so infallible as he liked to believe, Spilsbury continued his tireless work on behalf of law enforcement and forensic medicine.

This work ended in 1947. On December 19 one of Spilsbury's colleagues saw a light in the great man's laboratory. There was nothing unusual in this. Spilsbury often worked half the night. Then the colleague smelled gas. He tried the door. Locked.

Precious time was wasted locating the caretaker to open the door. Inside, Sir Bernard Spilsbury was found dead by his own hand of carbon monoxide poisoning.

He was seventy and had given his entire life to forensic pathology. Having suffered from two strokes and feeling his mental powers were ebbing, he chose to end his career.

A remarkable one it was. Spilsbury participated in so

many famous investigations, his findings and testimony often being crucial to the conviction, that it is difficult sometimes to decide whether he or another detective played the major role.

Most writers cite Dew as the man who solved the Crippen murder, but it seems unlikely he could have obtained a conviction without the brilliant work of Sir Bernard Spilsbury, the world's first great criminal pathologist.

ARTHUR
FOWLER
NEIL

 |||||

The man who couldn't be fooled

† Joseph Crossley, who owned a boarding house in Blackpool on the Irish seacoast of England, was greatly intrigued by a news story in his weekly copy of *The News of the World*. In mounting excitement he reread the item:

> Particularly sad circumstances under which a bride of a day met her death were investigated at an Islington inquest on Margaret Elizabeth Lloyd, thirty-eight, wife of a land agent of Holloway. The husband said he was married to deceased at Bath. After traveling to London, she complained of headache and giddiness,

and he took her to a medical man, who prescribed for her. The following morning she said she felt much better and during the day she went out shopping. At 7:30, she said she would have a bath, and she then appeared cheerful. A quarter of an hour later witness went out, and returned at a quarter past eight, expecting to see her in the sitting room. As she was not there, he inquired of the landlady, and they went to the bathroom, which was in darkness. He lit the gas, and then found his wife under the water, the bath being three parts full. The next day witnesses found a letter amongst the deceased's clothing, but there was nothing in it to suggest that she was likely to take her life.

Dr. Bates said death was due to asphyxia from drowning. Influenza, together with a hot bath, might have caused an attack of syncope.

That news item, which he saw at Christmas time in 1914, had special significance for Crossley. Just a little over a year previously a strikingly similar death had occurred to the wife of one of his tenants. At the time, Crossley had thought the death most peculiar. Now to have a second, nearly identical drowning—well, it was possible, he supposed. Still, there are some things beyond belief.

After mulling it over awhile, Crossley decided it was his duty as a citizen to call this coincidence to the attention of the proper authorities. Thus, the boarding house proprietor wrote to Scotland Yard in London, sending the clipping he had just read together with a clipping reporting the death which had occurred in his own boarding house. It read:

Bride's Sudden Death. Drowned after seizure in a hot bath. Mrs. George Smith, of 80 Kimberley Road, Portsmouth, who was married only six weeks ago, died suddenly in a Blackpool boardinghouse. Her husband, giving evidence at the inquest on Saturday, said he was of independent means. He met his wife, who was a nurse, three months ago, and six weeks ago they were married. Last Wednesday they traveled to Blackpool and engaged a room at 16 Regent Road.

During the journey, his wife complained of headache, and, as she was not better on arrival, she saw a doctor. On Friday night she took a hot bath. She was a considerable time in the bath, and he called to her. There was no answer. He entered the bathroom and found his wife lying in the water, dead.

Dr. Billing stated that a post-mortem showed that the heart was enlarged and affected. He concluded that the heat of the water had acted on the heart and caused a fit or a faint and in her helplessness she was drowned.

The clippings, together with Crossley's letter, were received at Scotland Yard, then sent to the station at Kentish Town marked "Suspicious Deaths. For Your Information, Action and Report." Since the house in which Mrs. Lloyd had died was at 14 Bismarck Road, Highgate, it fell in the precinct of Detective-Inspector Arthur Fowler Neil.

Tall and lean, Neil was another of the seemingly inexhaustible supply of crack detectives Scotland Yard seems able to produce. He was by reputation tireless— able, his colleagues maintained, to work twenty-four hours without sleep or flagging energy, then follow it with another twenty-four at equal efficiency.

Neil had to agree with Crossley that the two clippings formed an unnatural coincidence, and in January, 1915, he began his investigation of the most recent death. He talked to Mrs. Flint, who operated the boarding house at 14 Bismarck Road. She described Lloyd as a medium-sized, athletic-looking man between forty and fifty. His only unusual facial feature was his "keen eyes," as she described them.

Mrs. Flint told Neil that Lloyd had leased bedroom and bath, with living room privileges, after carefully inspecting the bathroom. That very night of December 17, 1914, as Mrs. Flint recalled it, Lloyd had asked her to recommend a doctor, saying his wife was not feeling well. The landlady had sent him and Mrs. Lloyd to see Dr. Bates. The following day Mrs. Lloyd seemed to be feeling better and, as she set out for an afternoon stroll, asked that a bath be prepared for that evening.

When she and Lloyd returned at seven-thirty, the tub was drawn, and Mrs. Flint went into the kitchen. Shortly thereafter she heard splashing in the tub and then, a few minutes later, someone playing the harmonium in the living room. The song—how could Mrs. Flint ever forget it—was *Nearer, My God to Thee*. She surmised that Lloyd had stayed in the living room while his wife was bathing.

Minutes later the doorbell rang. Mrs. Flint answered and was surprised to see Lloyd outside. He had gone out for tomatoes for their supper, he explained, and had forgotten his key. "I'm so sorry to have troubled you," he said, bowing.

"Not at all, Mr. Lloyd. Not at all."

"Has my wife come down to the living room yet?" he asked.

"No, I haven't seen her."

Lloyd looked puzzled and bounded upstairs.

Mrs. Flint had hardly returned to the kitchen when she heard Lloyd crying for help. She raced upstairs just as Lloyd was raising his wife from the bathtub. "Get the doctor," he cried. "Hurry!"

Dr. Bates came quickly, but he could not help. Mrs. Lloyd had drowned.

"Where is Lloyd now?" Neil asked.

"I have no idea. He stayed only long enough to settle

the formalities—there was an inquest, you know—then he moved out."

Neil inspected the bedroom, which was on the top floor, and the bath, which was off the stair landing, a flight down. The principal fixture was an iron tub which Neil carefully measured as fifty inches long at the bottom and sixty-six at the top. It was difficult to see how a grown person could accidentally drown in it.

The detective next consulted Dr. Bates. Yes, he remembered Mrs. Lloyd. She had come in with her husband, who had done all the talking. She didn't feel well, he explained, and was tired much of the time. Dr. Bates had agreed that she seemed rather lethargic and concluded that she was feverish. He had prescribed appropriate medication.

"What about the accident in the tub, Doctor?" Neil asked.

"There could be no doubt the woman drowned. There was white foam at her mouth—an unmistakable sign." He shook his head sadly. "She must have suffered an attack of weakness, slid beneath the water and drowned."

"Were there any bruises or marks of violence—anything to indicate there might have been a struggle?"

"No," said Dr. Bates, "I could find nothing of that sort. Later when I did the autopsy I found a small bruise above the left elbow—but that is hardly an indication of a struggle. It probably resulted from some compulsive movement as she tried to save herself."

Neil stood up and thanked the physician.

"I realize, Inspector, you want another report from me—but I've told you the truth." He paused, obviously trying as hard as he could to think of something. "Oh, there was one thing that was—well, strange, you might say. Lloyd showed no grief. He ordered the cheapest coffin. 'When they're dead, they're dead,' he said. It was hardly decent, if you ask me."

"Well, that may be helpful," said Neil, extending his hand. "If you should hear anything more from or about Lloyd, please let me know."

Intrigued and mystified, Neil pursued the case. He learned that Mrs. Lloyd was the former Margaret Elizabeth Lofty, the middle-aged daughter of a clergyman, whom Lloyd had met at Bristol and married at Bath.

Another piece of information Neil acquired was that, prior to renting Mrs. Flint's accommodations, Lloyd had sought to rent from Miss Lokker, who ran a boarding house in Highgate. He had shown great interest in the Lokker bathtub, inquiring whether "someone could lie down in it." Miss Lokker considered him most strange and refused to rent to him.

Neil's net caught other facts. Mrs. Lloyd had made out a will, naming her husband as sole heir—not so strange in itself, except that the will was signed only three hours before her death. On that same afternoon she had drawn out her entire savings. Then, Neil scoured up the information that Lloyd had gotten in touch with an attorney named W. T. Davies on Uxbridge Road and given him his late wife's will "for settlement."

On January 12 Dr. Bates summoned Neil, explaining that the Yorkshire Insurance Company in Bristol had written him about Mrs. Lloyd's death. It seemed that on December 4, 1914, just prior to her marriage, the then-Miss Lofty had taken out an insurance policy for seven hundred pounds. The beneficiary was Lloyd.

Neil had an idea the insurance policy might afford a way to lay hands on Lloyd and asked Dr. Bates to delay his reply to the insurance company.

On January 21 Neil received an exhaustive report from the Blackpool police in response to his query about the death of Mrs. Smith in the Crossley boarding house. According to this report, Mr. George Joseph Smith, a gentleman from Portsmouth, had stopped, along with his wife Alice, a fat but pretty woman of twenty-five, at the boarding house of Mrs. Marsden. On learning the establishment had no bath, the Smiths had left.

Journeying to the Crossley place, Smith had taken a room, after inspecting the bathtub, which was located on the second floor above the kitchen. Late in the afternoon of that same day, Smith had asked Mrs. Crossley to recommend a doctor, explaining that Mrs. Smith was suffering from a severe headache brought on by the trip from Portsmouth. They had gone to Dr. George Billing, who had examined Mrs. Smith. He found some minor heart murmurs and prescribed some powders for her headache.

The following day, Mrs. Smith appeared well and greeted the Crossleys cordially as she went out for an airing with her husband. At six that night, she ordered a bath and at eight Smith went up to his room with his wife.

The Crossleys stayed in the kitchen and soon noticed a wet spot on the kitchen ceiling. Moments later the doorbell rang. Smith was outside. "I'm sorry to trouble you," he said, "but I had to run out to buy some eggs for breakfast. I'm afraid I forgot my key."

Smith then hurried upstairs and within moments was shouting, "Get a doctor! Get Dr. Billing—he knows her."

Dr. Billing had come and found Smith holding his wife's head above water, which was up to her chest. Since she was so very heavy, Smith and Billing had difficulty lifting her out of the tub to the floor. When interviewed by Blackpool police, Billing said he found no signs of violence. He admitted he had not spent much time examining Mrs. Smith and in fact was not sure whether her head was at the foot or the head of the tub. The coroner gave the case only cursory attention and ruled, "Heart failure in the bath. Accidental drowning." Smith vanished.

The report from the exceedingly thorough Blackpool police contained other information which pleased Neil very much. Mrs. Smith was the former Alice Burnham, whom Smith had met in Southsea, where she was employed as a private nurse to an elderly man. At that time she had only twenty-seven pounds in cash, but she had lent her father, Charles Burnham in Aston Clinton, a hundred pounds. Miss Burnham and Smith became engaged in a few days and in two months, on October 30, 1913, they were married. The day before the wedding, she had taken out an insurance policy for five hundred pounds on herself. Smith was the beneficiary.

Right after the wedding, Smith had demanded that his father-in-law repay the hundred pounds with interest —and she had threatened to sue her father if he did not pay back the loan. Certainly, Smith was able to communicate his avarice to his wife.

On December 8, Mrs. Smith made out a will naming her husband as heir. Two days later, the couple left for Blackpool and in two more days she was dead.

To Neil the coincidences of the two "drownings" could only mean that Smith and Lloyd were the same man. Proving that they were was his second problem. The first was to find either one of them.

Neil figured he could flush out his man and asked Dr. Bates to send a favorable report to the insurance company on the death of Mrs. Lloyd. Neil's hope was that Lloyd would get in touch with his lawyer, Davies, as soon as he heard the insurance company was ready to pay off. With this in mind, Neil put the attorney's office under surveillance. Day and night the watch continued, until on February 1, 1915, a man who fitted the description of both Lloyd and Smith approached Davies' office.

Neil intercepted him. "I am Detective-Inspector Neil, London Metropolitan Police. Are you John Lloyd?"

"I am."

Neil droned on in the customary understatement of the English detectives. "The same John Lloyd whose wife was drowned in a bath on the night of December 18 last, at Bismarck Road, Highgate?"

"That's me."

"From my investigation I have reason to believe you are identical with George Joseph Smith, whose wife was found drowned in a bath in Blackpool in 1913. You married Miss Lofty, your last bride, at Bath, Bristol, under the name of Lloyd."

Lloyd appeared exasperated. "My name's not Smith. I don't know the name of Smith."

Neil hesitated a moment, or as he later put it, "I studied him. To this day it has always been a poser to me what women see in a man of this type. Sallow complexion, bad features, a big sensual mouth, in fact, the sort of fellow a decent man would shun at once as unlikable."

Neil was not impressed by Lloyd's denial and, affecting his best cop's manner, said, "I'm going to detain you for making a false attestation on oath to a registrar."

Lloyd seemed surprised. "Oh, if that's what all the fuss is over, I may as well tell you. Yes, I'm Smith and, yes, my wife died at Blackpool. But what of it? The entry in the marriage register is wrong, but that's all you got on me."

"The question of further charges is under investigation," replied Neil.

"I'll admit, Inspector, the two deaths were a remarkable coincidence," he said, grinning, "but that's my hard luck."

Plain fact was that unless Neil could discover how Smith-Lloyd had murdered his two wives, the minor charge of false attestation, under which he was now being held, was all Scotland Yard was apt to pin on him.

The "medical side" of the investigation was turned over to Dr. Bernard Spilsbury who, on February 4, went out to the cemetery at Islington to participate in the exhumation of Margaret Elizabeth Lloyd, Smith's last victim.

Spilsbury went over the body inch by inch looking for evidence of violence. There was none, except for the insignificant bruise on the elbow which Dr. Bates had noticed. Spilsbury examined the body for the slightest sign of heart or circulatory disease which might have caused her death. He even took samples of internal organs to test for poisons. But all of this was in the nature of extra precaution, because the evidence the woman had drowned was rather unmistakable. Foam at her mouth, swelling of the lungs with air, and other signs all pointed to this. She was not killed elsewhere and put in the tub to make it look like a drowning. Margaret Elizabeth Lloyd had drowned.

But how? How could an adult, healthy woman be forcibly drowned in a bathtub without there being any marks on the body? There would be bruises on the head, shoulders, arms, legs, as the woman struggled against the hands seeking to force her under the water. But there were no marks. How was it possible? Spilsbury asked Neil to have the tub transferred from Mrs. Flint's place on Bismarck Road to the Kentish Town station.

The first news stories of the autopsy appeared on February 5, and two days later the newspapers began to speak of the deaths as the "Brides in the Baths" case

Once again newspaper publicity played an important role, and on February 8 a letter arrived from the Police Chief of Herne Bay. He had read of the deaths Neil was investigating and thought he ought to tell him of a drowning that had occurred in Herne Bay on July 13, 1912.

In this case, a man named Henry Williams had rented a one-family house on High Street on May 20, 1912, for himself and his wife, Bessie, about thirty. Seven weeks later, on July 9, 1912, Williams bought a bathtub from an ironmonger. The following day Williams and his wife called at the office of a Dr. French, who was told that Mrs. Williams had suffered an attack of epilepsy. Dr. French prescribed a bromide.

On July 12 French was summoned in the middle of the night by Williams, who said his wife had had another seizure. Dr. French treated her and called again at three o'clock the next afternoon to find Mrs. Williams in good health.

The following morning Dr. French was again called to the house on High Street, where he found Mrs. Williams in the bathtub on her back, her head under the water. A cake of soap was clutched in her right hand. Her legs were stretched out straight, her feet protruding above the water at the lower end of the tub. French pronounced her dead. The coroner held a hasty inquest and since there were no signs of violence, ruled it was an accidental drowning during an epileptic seizure.

Neil read the report with both fascination and horror, dispatched pictures of Smith-Lloyd to Herne Bay, then went with Spilsbury to Blackpool to participate in the exhumation of the body of Mrs. Smith. Although that body was somewhat more decayed than Mrs. Lloyd's, Spilsbury again could find no signs of violence, while being confronted with many signs of drowning. Analysis had also ruled out the possibility of poison. Drowning it had to be. It was almost as if the adoring brides had drowned themselves just to please and make wealthy their husbands. Meanwhile, the second bathtub was transferred to Kentish Town station.

Neil now began the investigation of the drowning at Herne Bay, where witnesses had sworn that Smith-Lloyd was likewise Williams. The details of his swindle differed only slightly. Smith had met Bessie Mundy in Clifton, a suburb of Bristol, in 1910 and had been attracted to the 2,750 pounds which her father had left her. The inheritance was administered by a relative, however, who would permit her to receive only the interest, eight pounds a month.

By 1910 the interest had accumulated to 138 pounds and was available to Bessie at any time. On August 26, 1910, the day Williams married her, he demanded the

138 pounds. She gave it to him and he promptly vanished. Heartbroken, she returned to the spinster life.

Then in February, 1912, while staying in a boarding house at Weston-super-Mare, she ran into her erstwhile but still adored husband, forgave him on the spot and followed him to Herne Bay.

On July 2 Williams asked a lawyer whether he would inherit his wife's fortune after her death. Assured he would, he induced her to draw up a will. A day later Williams bought the bathtub, and three days later Bessie was dead.

Again a body was exhumed from its grave, and on February 19 Spilsbury examined the corpse. It was in an advanced stage of decomposition, but again there were no marks of violence and clear indications of drowning. The third tub was moved to Kentish Town.

Neil worked tirelessly. He visited over forty towns in England and interviewed over a hundred and fifty people running down Smith and his incredible *amours*. It seemed he had known and swindled many women, most of whom were still too embarrassed to talk about it. Whether there were other unreported deaths by drowning was hard to say.

Smith—that was his real name—was a most unsavory character. He was born in 1872, the son of an insurance agent. By age nine he had been sent to a reformatory and had spent much of the rest of his life in jail for fraud, swindling and theft. He was illiterate, common in speech, a bully and totally without a friend of his own sex, yet for some reason he had a phenomenal capacity to attract women—a talent which never ceased to amaze men.

Neil knew none of his labor was to be useful unless he could prove Smith murdered his wives. At the moment Smith was merely a not-very-nice fellow who profited from his three wives' deaths—but a murderer he was not —yet.

Spilsbury pondered the deaths. He went daily to Kentish Town and peered at the three iron tubs, as if hoping they would suddenly speak to reveal their secrets. He studied the measurements he had made of the three victims and tried to figure how they had drowned without evidence of violence. It was indeed a puzzle.

At Spilsbury's suggestion, Neil began some experiments with the tubs. He filled them with water and recruited a nurse who was an experienced swimmer and diver. He had her sit in the tubs in various positions while he tried to force her head under the water in a nonviolent way.

Neil discovered that if he pushed the nurse's head under the water she immediately clutched the sides of the tub with her arms and kicked and rolled over. There was a great thrashing about, and only the greatest force could have kept the nurse under long enough to drown. Likewise, if he tried to hold her body and head under, a struggle resulted. Every method Neil tried seemed certain to cause bruises. The mystery of the Brides in the Baths only deepened.

Then one day as Spilsbury was pondering the fate of Bessie Williams he had a thought. Bessie had supposedly died by an epileptic seizure. Spilsbury knew the first stage of an epileptic fit consists of a contraction of the entire body. If this is what had happened to Bessie, it was impossible for the five-foot, seven-inch woman to have drowned in her five-foot-long tub. If she had gone rigid in a seizure, her head would have been pushed up the sloping part of the tub, far above the level of the water.

The second part of an epileptic seizure is a violent spasm of the limbs during which they are drawn close to the body, then flung outward. This would virtually preclude any drowning. Her arms would catch on the side of the tub and keep her from going under. Nor could she drown in the third or relaxed phase of the seizure, for she was just too big for the tub.

Yet, Dr. French had said that Bessie Williams' head was under the water, her legs extended and her feet protruding above the water. There was no way this could have happened, unless— Spilsbury had an idea, which he passed on to Neil.

The following day Neil tried a new experiment. As the nurse was sitting in the tub, he suddenly grabbed her by the ankles and abruptly jerked her feet out of the water. Her head went under before she had a chance to grab the sides of the tub or to struggle in any way.

A second later Neil noticed—to his horror—the nurse was not moving. Quickly he pulled her shoulders out of the water and her head fell limply to the side. A half hour of frantic work by a doctor and a distraught detective was needed to bring her back to consciousness.

When she came to at last, she remembered only that as she slid down in the bath, water rushed up her nose. At that instant she had lost consciousness. She had, as Spilsbury explained, gone into shock despite the fact that, unlike Smith's victims, she had anticipated Neil's actions and was an experienced swimmer and diver.

Neil's graphic descriptions of his experiments to the jurors made them shudder. They needed only twenty minutes to find Smith guilty of murder, and on June 30, 1915, he was sentenced to hang, and this sentence was carried out.

After the jury rendered its verdict, the judge said, "This conviction, a thoroughly right one in my opinion, is largely due to the care and assiduity with which Inspector Neil has pursued the threads of this complicated case, and I have the pleasure of saying so in public."

ELMER
LINCOLN
IREY

The gentle crime fighter

† One by one, seven men entered a one-story brick building at 2122 North Clark Street in Chicago. The letters on the plate-glass window said it was the S.M.C. Cartage Co. Actually it was the central garage for the George "Bugs" Moran bootlegging operation. Those who entered the building were five members of the Moran gang, a fifty-dollar-a-week mechanic who maintained the seven trucks used by the gang, and Dr. Reinhardt H. Schwimmer, an optometrist who liked to hang around hoodlums. The date was February 14—Valentine's Day —1929.

Shortly after the seventh man entered the building, three men burst in, wearing policemen's uniforms, guns drawn. One of them barked: "Okay, you guys. Up against the wall."

"Say, what is this?" one of Moran's men snarled. "Who are you birds? You're new in this district?"

"Never mind who we are. Turn around. Put your hands over your head and against the wall." To show he meant business he leveled his revolver menacingly.

In disbelief, almost in amusement, the Moran boys complied. They knew cops couldn't make any charges stick. "Oh, brother," smirked one, "just wait till George gets here. He'll have you chumps so far out in the sticks it'll take you two days to get home."

At that moment the door opened again, and two men in bulky civilian overcoats, but with stars pinned to their lapels, entered. The men in uniform stood aside, and the newcomers threw open their coats and brought out sub-machine guns.

Deliberate, unhurried, the machine gunners went to work on the seven men lined up against the wall. Firing in unison, one man sprayed bullets from left to right— head high, while the other fired from right to left, aiming at the neck and shoulders. Twice more the gunners criss-crossed, aiming slightly lower each time. The final bursts raked the crumpling bodies at the knee joints.

This, the infamous St. Valentine's Day Massacre, was the climax of one of the more incredible eras in the history of crime. Now, almost forty years later, the lawlessness and savagery of the 1920's defy belief.

Gambling, prostitution and other forms of vice had always existed in cities all over the world. In America these activities were tolerated with less resignation, perhaps, but they existed nonetheless. They led to the customary graft and corruption of police and officials and to gang warfare and "unsolved" murders. Some cities were worse than others, but in the main, racketeering and the attendant evils were under some form of control.

Then, in 1920, in a wave of idealistic fervor, the country outlawed the manufacture, sale, transportation, importation or exportation of alcoholic beverages. It was "prohibition." The nation went "dry," hoping thereby to eliminate alcoholism as a disease and to eradicate crime, vice, debauchery in its various forms, idleness, waste and a wide variety of other evils which decades of somewhat specious propaganda had led a large segment of the population to believe were associated with "drink."

The effect of prohibition was something else entirely. It became the greatest imaginable boon to lawlessness. The law itself was partly to blame. It made it illegal to manufacture, sell and transport intoxicants—but it said nothing about their consumption. The man who drank the illegally manufactured, transported and sold liquor was not breaking the law, so he crowded into "speakeasies" to imbibe illegal liquor—legally. Going to the speakeasy became the fashionable thing to do. Millions did it regularly, feeling rather daring. And, having crossed over the line into lawlessness, they decided to go a little further, place a few bets, visit a casino or engage in some form of vice. The whole country, reacting to the blood and toil of World War I, went on a lawbreaking spree.

For the gangsters it was payday every day. They could manufacture and sell any alcoholic product and charge what the traffic would bear. They paid no liquor taxes and bought no tavern or cabaret licenses. The profits were staggering. In 1923, Johnny Torrio and Al Capone, two Chicago mobsters, shared a profit of over seven million dollars from operations in that city and environs. That was only the beginning. By 1926, Chicago had twenty thousand speakeasies. There were three thousand bawdy houses, three hundred major gambling emporiums and two thousand bookie joints. A year later, Al Capone was estimated to have annual revenue of sixty million dollars from bootlegging, twenty-five million from gambling, ten million from vice and fifteen million from labor racketeering—and his was only one of several gangs operating in the city.

The gangsters used their illegal income to spawn further evil. At the height of its power, the Capone mob elected the mayor of Chicago and then named the chief of police. Judges, prosecutors, scores of police offices in Chicago, suburban towns, and the state of Illinois were bought—thus enabling the speakeasies, gambling dens and brothels to operate openly on public streets.

Gangs competed for power, for "territories," for sources of liquor and guns and the other paraphernalia of the empire of evil. In Chicago open warfare resulted. By actual count, 135 hoodlums were slain there in "unsolved" murders between 1923 and 1926. By the St. Valentine's Day Massacre in 1929, criminal violence and murder were like a plague on the nation. In one year alone there were 116 unexplained "bombings" in Chicago, and not one of them led to an arrest. The streets echoed to the rattle of machine guns—and the law was that of the jungle.

Chicago, the state of Illinois, even the federal government seemed powerless to stop the wave of crime. Minor hoodlums were occasionally arrested and convicted, but the crime overlords, men like Capone, remained untouchable. For example, where was Capone when his "boys" perpetrated the St. Valentine's Day Massacre? He was at his Florida estate, basking in the sunshine. In ordering the murders, he was guilty of murder. But how could he be convicted when he was two thousand miles away, when all who saw the murders were dead, and when the actual gunmen knew that if they opened their mouths they would be dead?

Capone had gotten away with murders, assaults, extortions, robberies and racketeering, but on St. Valentine's Day, 1929, he went too far. Responsible citizens of Chicago, seeing their city being destroyed by a man dubbed the "millionaire gorilla," gathered a fund of seventy-five thousand dollars to fight him. The men who gave the money were called the "Secret Six." At the same time, President Herbert Hoover, inaugurated shortly after the massacre, issued orders for Capone somehow to be put in jail.

There was, theoretically at least, one way for the federal government to "get" Capone—income tax evasion. The pudgy gangster obviously had a great deal of money. He bought the best suits by the half-dozen and had extra-deep gun pockets tailored into them. He shopped for monogrammed silk shirts—a dozen at a time. He lived in a lavishly decorated house in Chicago, had an estate in Florida, and at both places threw lavish parties for hundreds of guests, supplying food, drink and entertainment on a royal scale. He rode in a seven-ton armored limousine and was always surrounded by a small battalion of aides, servants, bodyguards, lieutenants and henchmen.

Capone was hardly poverty stricken, yet he had never filed an income tax form in his life. There could be no doubt he had evaded payment of income taxes. Income tax evasion had already been used to jail Capone's brother, Ralph "Bottles" Capone. Perhaps it would work against the big man himself. Attempting to jail Al in this way was an irony, indeed, for of all Capone's crimes, non-payment of taxes was the least vicious. But it might —just might—put him behind bars.

The task of getting Capone for income tax evasion fell to the Intelligence Division of the Internal Revenue Service, headed by Chief Elmer Lincoln Irey. He was one of the first and certainly best of the new type of "cop" who would transform modern law enforcement.

Typical of the new breed, Irey had never walked a beat or swung a billy club or performed any of the tasks of the uniformed policeman or police detective. Born in Kansas City in 1888 and reared in Washington, D.C., he attended public high school and Georgetown Law School. His real talent was as a stenographer. At eighteen he was secretary to the president of the Washington Railway and Electric Company, and at nineteen he became a clerk in the office of the Chief Post Office Inspector. This background would make a veteran cop sneer, even when Irey became a full-fledged postal inspector before he was thirty.

In 1919, when he was thirty-one, Irey became chief of a handful of postal inspectors chosen to form the Intelligence Service of the Internal Revenue Service. The United States has always used a voluntary or honor system to collect income taxes. Citizens are asked to declare their income, figure their own tax and pay it. The overwhelming majority of Americans do this—but there are, inevitably, some cheats. The intelligence unit was set up to see that the cheats paid their taxes like everyone else.

As he set out to make Capone pay his taxes, Irey, at forty-two, was the exact opposite of the boisterous, brutal, high-living Capone. A kind, gentle man, devoted to his family, Irey was repelled by violence, almost incapable of hate. He even spoke kindly of Capone, an attitude which amazed the Chicago gangster.

In his first act in the campaign against Capone, Irey, in March, 1930, went to Chicago and mapped strategy with Arthur P. Madden, agent-in-charge of the Chicago office of the Intelligence Service. It was quickly apparent that the task of getting Capone would not be easy. He was much smarter than his brother Ralph or even his lieutenants, Frank "The Enforcer" Nitti and Sam Guzik, both of whom were nabbed on income tax raps.

Capone put nothing in writing and paid only cash. All his property was listed under aliases or dummy corporations. He was a careful man who ostensibly made no money and spent none. Proving that he evaded income taxes would take some doing.

After listening to Madden's recital, Irey took advantage of the fact that he was a stranger in Chicago and checked into the Lexington Hotel, Capone's headquarters. He spent two days sitting in the lobby and moving through the hotel, soaking up the flavor of the place, taking the temper of the hoodlums who hung around it.

Returning to Washington, Irey decided the only way he could gather evidence on Capone was to infiltrate the organization. The undercover agent would not only have to look, act, smell, and dress like a hoodlum. He would need a criminal record, a history of gangland associations, encyclopedic knowledge of criminals and their crimes—plus brains, alertness, nerves of steel and almost superhuman courage.

Amazingly Irey had such a man, perhaps the single most astounding detective of modern times. For decades he infiltrated one vicious gang of hoodlums after another. He gave up wife, child, privacy, security and nearly everything else he valued in single-minded dedication to law enforcement. He was officially known as "Pat O'Rourke," but that was just a cover name. His real identity was never revealed so long as he lived. In fact, only one or two top men in the Intelligence Service knew his real identity. He seldom appeared in Washington and then only under the strictest security. He was Michael J. Malone, whose fantastic story may never be told because he took no notes and made only the sketchiest reports of his cases.

It was Malone, an Irishman, whom Irey turned to as undercover agent. Malone had a wonderful ability to look and talk like an Italian, Jew, Greek or whatever ethnic origin was needed. He was easy to meet, easy to talk to, easy to take for granted. No one objected to having him around. Irey knew Malone would need these qualities— and much more. He would need an identity. So Irey sent him to Philadelphia and then to Brooklyn, to talk to informers and imbibe the necessary underworld lore.

Late in 1930 Malone took the train for Chicago. Outfitted with an expensive wardrobe financed with part of the seventy-five-thousand-dollar "Secret Six" Fund, he registered at the Lexington Hotel. Casual, relaxed, he hung around the hotel, reading, having a drink, writing an occasional letter. He noticed some of Capone's men watching him and figured he had made a favorable impression.

Soon one man sidled up to him. "What's your line, Jack?"

Malone looked the stranger over carefully. "I'm a promoter," he said, grinning. "Know anybody who'd be interested in buyin' some gold bricks?"

The gangster laughed. "Come on upstairs. We'd like to talk to you."

Malone joined his new friends in a drink. "What goes on here?" he asked. "Do you guys run the hotel and check on everybody who holes in here?"

"We just like to know who's around—just to make sure they ain't dicks."

Malone took a sip of his drink. "So, what's on your mind?"

"I see you registered St. Louis as your home town. That on the level?"

Malone pretended to be cautious, looking his two new friends over carefully, "What do you want to know for?"

The answer pleased Capone's men. They liked a close-mouthed guy. "You look like you might be on the lam," said one of them. "If you was open to a proposition—we might have somethin' for you."

Malone allowed as how he might be interested.

"Okay," said the gangster. "So you ain't from St. Louis. Where you from?"

"Brooklyn."

The word was magic, for Capone had cut his criminal eyeteeth in the New York borough.

"You from Brooklyn! Why you on the lam?"

Malone then described a shooting in Brooklyn which he knew would never be solved, yet which the Capone people had heard about. His story seemed to impress them, and they promised to get back to him in a couple of days.

The next week was the longest in Irey's life as he waited for Capone's men to check out Malone's cover. He knew the gangsters would thoroughly investigate Malone's phony Brooklyn contacts. If they spotted them as false, the agent was as good as dead.

Eventually, Malone was called into the two gangsters' room. "We've been checkin' on you." They grinned. It could have meant anything. "You've been a bad boy—and we got a proposition for you."

"What kind of proposition?" Malone tried to appear noncommittal.

"We'll go into that later. First you gotta meet the boys and see how they like you."

The meeting was to take place at a big banquet to be held shortly.

Irey lived a thousand mental tortures in the next few days. He knew that Capone would get great satisfaction out of stringing Malone along and then, at the height of the banquet, calling him forward, revealing him as a betrayer, beating him senseless on the spot and later "disposing" of him. Irey felt responsible for Malone. If anything happened to him—

Malone passed his test handsomely. He met Capone at the banquet, and they chatted amiably. The job he was given was as croupier in the big Capone gambling casino in the Hawthorne Hotel in Cicero, a Chicago suburb. This would put him right in the midst of Capone operations. He would be around most of the big-shots.

At the same time that Irey sent Malone to Chicago to infiltrate Capone's organization, he sent an agent, unknown in Chicago, to be his contact. This was Frank John Wilson, also destined to be a great name in federal law enforcement, a man who would become chief of the Secret Service.

When Wilson arrived in Chicago in 1930, he set up offices apart from the regular Intelligence Service offices. He and Irey and Arthur Madden took elaborate precautions to avoid being seen together. At the same time a communications system was set up. The telephones of more than fifty top Capone men and their girl friends were tapped and all the taps fed into one switchboard. The setup was financed by the "Secret Six."

The telephone taps paid a dividend two days before

Christmas, 1930, when a snatch of conversation was overheard. It went like this:

"Snorky's gonna have that fella taken care of."

"How? When?"

"Search me."

"Where's he livin', anyway?"

"The S.P."

The seemingly unintelligible words sent chills through Intelligence agents, for they knew "Snorky" was one of Capone's nicknames and the "S.P." stood for the Sheridan Plaza Hotel, where Frank Wilson was living. Somehow Capone's men had spotted Wilson as an agent. Irey almost called off the entire investigation. Not only was Wilson endangered, but chances were that if Wilson was spotted, so was Malone.

Irey managed to get word of the phone call to Malone and asked him to try to learn what Capone was up to— and particularly if he was in danger himself. Malone's report—delivered by letter, the one means of communication Capone could not tamper with—was that Wilson was in danger. Malone did not feel he himself was under suspicion. Irey wanted to recall Wilson to protect him, but Wilson insisted on staying on the job.

Shortly after New Year's, 1931, Malone became involved in a conversation with one of Capone's hoodlums, the gist of which was that the "income tax dicks" weren't so smart. They'd had in their possession for over five years a record book that could send Capone to jail— only they were too dumb to realize it. Capone had been worried for a while, but now he figured the federal men would never wise up.

This information puzzled Arthur Madden. He could think of no such record or ledger or other document. Wilson, who had been poring over all the seized Capone financial records for months, had seen nothing. But he went through everything again, just to make sure.

Thus it was that after a few days of sifting through boxes of documents, Wilson noticed a ledger marked "Barracks, Burnham, Ill." This was a Capone-operated brothel. The record book could hardly be significant. But opening it, Wilson saw that the Burnham title was phony and that the figures inside indicated a far larger operation. There were references to horse bets, dice, roulette and other games. On nearly every page there were notations of large sums paid to "Al." Al could only be Capone himself. If this was so, the ledger could be the long-sought proof that Capone had received income which he failed to report.

Investigation revealed that the ledger had been seized in a 1926 raid on the Hawthorne Smoke Shop, a large

Capone gambling emporium in the Hawthorne Hotel in Cicero, Illinois, the very place where Malone now toiled as a croupier.

Irey knew that for the ledger to be accepted as proof in court, his men would have to find the bookkeeper and convince him to testify that he had made the notations and that "Al" referred to Al Capone. Who had been Capone's accountant? After five years he was probably dead. Capone would most likely eliminate anyone who could incriminate him.

Irey had to find out who this accountant was. He sent to Chicago a handwriting expert, who decided that two different men had made entries in the ledger. The expert compared the handwriting with that of every known underworld bookkeeper and Capone agent. The result was zero. The handwriting samples could not be identified. Again Irey and Wilson had reached a blind alley. Unless—it was a chance, but maybe Malone could come up with some additional information. It meant asking questions—and asking questions was often fatal for any hoodlum, let alone an undercover agent.

Malone had so effectively put himself beyond suspicion that he was able to discover the names of the two accountants—Les Shumway and Fred Reis. Capone had tried to find both to kill them but had never succeeded.

If Capone failed, could Irey do better? He sent agents fanning throughout the Chicago area, and after a week of footwork they located the flea-bitten rooming house where Shumway had lived while working at the Hawthorne Smoke Shop. Yes, the landlady remembered Mr. Shumway. He had hated Chicago's winters and gone south—oh, back in 1925. Did she know where? Oh, my, no—wait, she had forwarded a couple of Mr. Shumway's letters to a hotel in Miami. She didn't remember which one.

Wilson went to Miami to track the missing accountant. This was a most risky undertaking, for Capone was in Miami at that time, too, and the Florida resort crawled with his gunmen. They would like nothing better than to eliminate Wilson. Before letting him go, Irey insisted he wear dark glasses and make some effort to disguise himself.

Danger or no, Wilson began checking second-rate hotels, rooming houses, underworld contacts in Miami. His efforts produced only the scant tip that Shumway might be working at Hialeah Race Track. It was bearding the lion in his den to go there, for Capone was in almost daily attendance at the track, but Wilson went anyway. Studying the employees there, he finally narrowed the possible Shumways down to three and arranged to have each secretly photographed. The photos were sent to Chicago and shown to Shumway's landlady, who picked out one as her former tenant.

Wilson followed Shumway to his hotel room and confronted him there. At first he refused to talk. He had survived Capone's threats and right now existed under Capone's nose at the race track simply because Capone didn't know him personally; those of Capone's men who did know him had all been eliminated in Chicago's incessant gang warfare. No, Shumway didn't want any trouble.

Wilson had a big weapon to use against Shumway. The government could subpoena him and force him to testify at Capone's trial. If this happened, how long did Shumway think Capone would let him live? Shumway's only chance, Wilson argued, was to cooperate with the government and rely on Treasury agents to protect him. The accountant asked for time to think.

That night Irey received word from Malone, who was still in his undercover role, that Capone's boys had spotted Shumway in Miami and were going to get him. Fearful for both Shumway and Wilson, Irey phoned his agent and told him to leave Miami with Shumway as soon as possible. At the same time, Irey stationed other agents outside Shumway's hotel to guard him.

Wilson went to see the fugitive accountant the next evening and persuaded him to leave—right then! None too soon. Agents parked outside the hotel saw a car full of Capone's thugs pull up in front of the hotel and race inside—only minutes after Wilson and Shumway departed.

Not long afterward Fred Reis, the accountant, was found hiding in southern Illinois. He, too, was persuaded to testify against Capone—out of fear that if he didn't he would be killed. The terror Capone had used so effectively was now being turned against him.

Shumway and Reis returned to Illinois and, hidden outside Chicago, were intensively questioned about the ledger. They testified to a federal grand jury, which in June, 1931, returned indictments against Capone for failure to file income tax statements and for attempting to evade payment of taxes. He was released in fifty thousand dollars bail.

Capone smirked and swaggered as he posted bail, but he was clearly worried—enough so to post a fifty-thousand-dollar price tag on the heads of Shumway, Reis, Wilson and Irey.

Irey took elaborate precautions to protect the lives of the two bookkeepers. Both were in the constant company of intelligence agents as they traveled, non-stop, about the country. Before they were brought back to Chicago to testify to the grand jury, Irey had information planted that Reis was in Los Angeles and Shumway in Baltimore. Capone dispatched a squad of his goons to each city, thus lessening the danger both men faced in Chicago. After the indictments were returned, Reis was put aboard a ship for South America to keep him safe until the trial, and Shumway, together with an agent, took a job in an isolated lumber camp in Oregon.

Capone was not finished, however. In September, 1931, a month before the trial, a well-dressed man walked into the New York office of Joseph H. Callan, an executive of the Crucible Steel Company. After identifying himself as a representative of Capone, he said, "You are one of Elmer Irey's closest friends. Your wife and Elmer Irey went to school together in Washington. Right?"

"That's right," said Callan, "but why have you gone to the trouble to learn all this?"

The visitor hesitated, as though for effect, then said, "We have one and a half million dollars in cash that we are willing to part with, if a compromise can be arranged so that Al stays out of jail. As Irey's friend, you arrange it. If Irey settles for a million—you can keep the other half million."

It was perhaps the largest bribe ever offered a law enforcement officer. Callan threw his visitor out of his office—bodily.

Soon another Capone emissary called upon Irey himself, with Capone's offer to pay a certain amount in back taxes and penalties, if he remained out of jail.

Irey replied in his usual soft-spoken manner, "I don't happen to share the fear that Al Capone throws into a great many people. As far as I am concerned Al Capone is just a big fat man in a mustard-colored suit."

Meanwhile, Mike Malone continued functioning in his undercover role—and a good thing he did. Worried, he reported that Capone had imported four gunmen from New York to assassinate Irey, Wilson, Madden and the principal witnesses. As the trial approached, the area around the Post Office Building in Chicago, where the Federal Court convened, resembled an armed camp. The New York boys never showed up.

Five days before the trial was to begin, Malone reported that Capone had gotten a list of the one hundred people selected as prospective jurors. "Al's boys are out interviewing them now," Malone said. "They've got dough, and they've got guns."

Worried, Irey went to see Judge James H. Wilkerson, who was to preside at the trial. The Judge listened and nodded, "Mr. Irey, don't you worry. Everything will be all right."

On the day of the trial Judge Wilkerson out-foxed Capone by bringing in a new list of prospective jurors—unreached by hoodlums.

The trial lasted eleven days, during which Mike Malone again delivered vital information. One of Capone's thugs was in the courtroom with a gun. The gangster was picked up and carried outside.

The jury deliberated ten hours and found Capone guilty on most counts brought by the government. Judge Wilkerson fined him fifty thousand dollars and ordered him to pay thirty thousand dollars in court costs. More important, Capone was sentenced to eleven years in prison.

Capone served his term, and his power was broken. He became ill from latent syphilis in prison. His mind deteriorated until his death in 1947.

In later years, income tax evasion would be used with regularity to bring to justice gangsters who figured they were too powerful or too clever to be caught for their "real" crimes.

Irey went on to an unparalleled career. As boss of the IRS Intelligence Service, he made a vital contribution to solution of the Lindbergh kidnapping. He cracked down on crooked political bosses as well as major criminals, successfully prosecuting Boss Pendergast in Kansas City and Huey Long in Louisiana for income tax evasion. So efficient did Irey and his men become in the prosecution of big-time criminals that they were dubbed the "giant killers."

In 1943 Irey was named to coordinate the activities of all Treasury agents, including the Secret Service and customs inspectors, as well as revenue agents. He retired in 1947 and died July 19, 1948.

JOHN
EDGAR
HOOVER

General of a great
detective army

† Christmas it may have been, but jolly it was not, as a half-dozen men armed with sub-machine guns, shotguns and pistols marched into the Third North-Western Bank in Minneapolis. After threatening the customers and employees, the gangsters scooped up all the money they could find and headed for the door.

A policeman suddenly appeared and fired. He was gunned down by a burst from a machine gun. Out in the street a second policeman opened fire. Another spurt of lead ended his life.

The hoodlums hopped into their car, carrying hostages on the running boards to prevent anyone from shooting. But an unarmed civilian was spotted. He seemed to be writing down the license number of the getaway car. A machine gun was raised, the trigger pressed. His life was taken, too.

It was another bank robbery by the Barker-Karpis gang of the 1930's, which for pure, wanton criminality has had few equals in this century. Its members killed ten people, wounded four and stole over a million dollars in cash, securities and other property during the more than five years they operated. But statistics cannot convey the terror, suffering and human waste they caused as they swept, guns chattering, through a dozen states.

Yet the nation owes a debt to "Ma" Barker and Alvin "Old Creepy" Karpis, for their gang and the others of the same era, those of Dillinger, "Baby Face" Nelson, "Pretty Boy" Floyd and "Machine Gun" Kelly, were the crucible which forged the Federal Bureau of Investigation.

Today the FBI is recognized as the finest law enforcement agency in the world. In size, authority, techniques, personnel, training, *esprit de corps*, numbers of arrests and convictions, the respect with which it is held and just about every other way the effectiveness of a police agency is measured, the FBI is the best there is.

Its 6,000 agents, in just one recent year alone, located 12,810 fugitives; recovered 19,856 stolen vehicles; recorded fines, savings and recoveries of stolen goods in the sum of $210,771,402; and produced evidence leading to the conviction of 12,921. These offenders were sentenced to prison terms totalling 38,196 years and fined $2,500,000!

The FBI has over 171 million fingerprints on file, operates the finest crime lab in the world and annually trains state and municipal police officers from all over the United States and many foreign countries. The accomplishments of the FBI in identifying and capturing criminals, spies, saboteurs, racketeers and other lawbreakers are already legend.

What is so incredible about the FBI is that it is to such a large extent the work of one man, John Edgar Hoover. He molded it, picked its men, trained them, set standards for them, led them out to do battle against crime, developed the techniques which made them so successful and established the administrative machinery to keep the Bureau functioning superbly year after year.

So successful is the FBI today that it is taken for granted. Its self-created image of smooth, dedicated, incorruptible and highly-efficient law enforcement tends to erase the fact it is made up of human beings or that it was ever anything but successful or that it had to struggle for its very existence against the likes of Ma Barker and Al Karpis.

When the Barker-Karpis and other Midwestern gangs burst on the scene in 1931, the country was simply not prepared to cope with them. They had automatic weapons which no civilians and few police forces could match. They had fast cars to carry them across state lines in minutes. Fast transportation plus instant communication by telephone enabled them to disperse and regroup quickly—just as in warfare. Finally, the gangs had a favorable public opinion behind them. No one openly praised them, but many people secretly admired their derring-do, their "fast life" with cars, guns, whiskey and women. Such attitudes were the residue of prohibition, when it became fashionable to flout the law and to know a "bootlegger" at a neighborhood "speakeasy."

Coping with the gangs required law enforcement which had proper transportation, communication, weapons—and authority to cross state lines in a hunt for lawbreakers. No city, state or even federal agency had the needed ability and authority. Certainly no one figured the FBI, a band of 325 agents, thinly spread over 48 states, was equal to the task. The FBI men were lawyers and accountants, rather than police officers, and they were unarmed. What could they do against a sub-machine gun?

Hoover figured his men could do a lot. When the Barker-Karpis gang began its criminal reign, Hoover had been FBI director for seven years. The organization he had taken over in 1924 had come a long way. Admittedly it had been next to useless when created out of the Secret Service in 1908 by President Theodore Roosevelt, the former "Rough Rider" and New York Police Commissioner. In 1912 President William Howard Taft had dignified it with the title of Bureau of Investigation in the Department of Justice. More than a title was needed. Its men, scorned as "briefcase" agents, had little legal authority against crime, and they were unable to protect the country against spies and saboteurs in World War I. In the early twenties the Bureau was rife with politics and scandal. If it was going to be saved at all, something drastic would have to be done soon.

On May 10, 1924, Attorney General Harlan Fiske Stone, soon to be an outstanding Supreme Court Justice, called in Hoover, then a twenty-nine-year-old assistant to the Attorney General, and gave him the job of cleaning up the Bureau of Investigation.

The choice of Hoover was startling in many ways. Aside from his youth, he was totally inexperienced. Born in Washington, D. C., on New Year's Day, 1895, he attended public schools and went to work in the Library of Congress in 1913, while attending the George Washington University Law School at night. When he received his law degree in 1916, he started to work in the Department of Justice as a $990-a-year lawyer. He had worked in the anti-subversion branch of the investigative bureau and at twenty-six had been made an assistant to the Attorney General. But to consider him the man to clean up the political mess in the Bureau of Investigation smacked of the foolish.

"I'll take the job," said Hoover, "on certain conditions."

"What are they?" the Attorney General asked.

"The Bureau must be divorced from politics and not be a catch-all for political hacks. Appointments must be based on merit. Second, promotions will be made on proven ability, and the Bureau will be responsible only to the Attorney General."

Stone beamed, then said, "I wouldn't give it to you under any other conditions."

With Stone's powerful backing and the keen interest of Herbert Hoover, the man soon to be elected President, J. Edgar Hoover started molding his organization. The political appointees went out, to be replaced with men like himself, lawyers (plus a few accountants) who were smart, tough, dedicated. He paid them well and gave them every opportunity for advancement; trained them to use guns, even though they still couldn't carry them; schooled them in the latest techniques of the underworld; and laid down rules against drinking or any behavior that would hurt public confidence in the agency. Thus, Hoover began to recruit and to fashion a new type of cop who was intelligent, educated, highly trained, dedicated, personally above criticism.

To cope with Ma Barker and her progeny, the FBI would need a lot more than that. Ma Barker was born Arizona "Kate" Clark in the Ozarks in 1872 of Scotch, Irish and, maybe, Indian parentage. When she was twenty, she married George Barker, a quiet, mild-mannered man, by whom she had four sons, Herman, Lloyd, Arthur, better known as "Dock," and Fred. Ma Barker was fiercely loyal to her sons. They could do no wrong, and when the young men got in trouble with the local law, which was frequently, she talked or scolded authorities out of "persecuting" her poor boys.

Soon more than scolding was needed. By the 1920's the boys had run the gamut of crime from larceny to murder. By 1930 Dock was serving a life term in Oklahoma State Prison for murder, Lloyd was in Leavenworth for mail robbery, and Freddie was in Kansas State Penitentiary for burglary and larceny. The only one not in jail was Herman—for he had committed suicide in 1927 rather than face arrest for burglary.

It is difficult to say when Ma Barker left her husband and joined her sons in planning and committing crimes, but certainly by March 30, 1931, when Freddie Barker was paroled from prison, the gang had been formed. Two months later a key member appeared when Fred's best prison buddy, Alvin Karpis, was paroled. Karpis' real name was Francis Albin Karpaviecz. Born in Canada in 1907 of Lithuanian parents, he was reared in Kansas. At nineteen he was sent to the Kansas Reformatory for robbery. He escaped but was picked up during a burglary and returned to prison. Released in 1931, he was twenty-four years old, tall, skinny, thin-featured, sallow-complexioned and pimply-faced with the vacant, droopy eyes of a very old or very demented man, which led to his nickname, "Old Creepy."

Ma Barker liked him immediately, treating him as her son, and the gang they formed remained an entity for five years. There were many personnel changes—for a number of very violent reasons—but it was both the first and the last of the great Midwestern gangs.

Freddie Barker and Karpis were hardly out of prison when they committed a robbery, using a DeSoto as the getaway car. Two days later, Sheriff C. R. Kelly of West Plains, Missouri, spotted the car in a garage and went over to question the two occupants. A blast from a shot-gun cut him down before he could draw his own weapon. The Barker-Karpis gang had committed its first murder.

Ma and the rest fled to St. Paul, where they lived quietly in a fashionable neighborhood. This served two purposes. It made a good hideout. Police didn't expect hoods like them to be in a swank setting. Then, Ma loved "nice things" and indulged these whims whenever pos-sible. A number of robberies and burglaries were pulled off without a hitch, for in those days the boys listened to Ma. She didn't like violence unless absolutely neces-sary, and she planned carefully to avoid it.

But Karpis and Freddie were not so squeamish about "rough stuff," as became evident on April 25, 1931, when the nude body of a man was found on the shores of a lake near Webster, Wisconsin. The body had been shot three times. The corpse was identified as that of Arthur V. "Old Man" Dunlop, a member of the gang.

FBI agents who came to the scene had no trouble figuring out what had happened. The gang's landlady had become suspicious of her tenants and had called police. Unfortunately her call was taken by a cop who was either dishonest or stupid, for six hours elapsed be-fore police raided the house. The gang was gone. Obvi-ously, they figured Dunlop had "fingered" them and disposed of him.

The gang fled to Kansas City, again settling into a posh neighborhood. After joining with some other bank robbers, they looted a bank at Fort Scott. But FBI agents were on their trail, and on July 7, 1932, agents stepped out from behind bushes at the Old Mission Golf Course and handcuffed three members of the gang. Unfortunately the arrest was seen by a fourth member of the gang, who went racing to Ma and Karpis. When agents arrived at the hideout, the gang had fled—right in the middle of dinner.

But the arrest led to another murder. The attorney who tried in vain to get the arrested gang members acquitted was found shortly afterward—full of holes.

The gang, now reduced to Ma, Freddie and Karpis, returned to St. Paul, where they moved into the wealthy Dellwood section as Mrs. Hunter and two sons. All summer they stayed there, arousing no suspicion, not even when a small, bald-headed man visited them. He was Frank "Jelly" Nash, a celebrated bank bandit. On July 26 Nash showed Freddie, Karpis and a few others how it was done, as they robbed the Cloud County Bank at Concordia, Kansas, of $240,000 in bonds and cash.

The money came in handy as Ma sought to win—or buy—freedom for her two other sons. She failed to get Lloyd out of Leavenworth, but Dock was paroled from Oklahoma on the condition that he never return to the state. That fall, Ma went to visit a sister in California, and while she was gone, the gang robbed the Minneapolis bank. Her careful planning was missed, for three men were killed. Some months later the outfit robbed the National Bank at Fairbury, Nebraska, of $151,350, this time without killing anyone. Ma had returned to advise them.

The character of the gang changed not long after that with the addition of Fred Goetz, college football star turned hoodlum. He had joined the Capone mob and become a proficient trigger man. It was believed he was one of the gunners in the St. Valentine's Day Massacre. Goetz was accompanied by his attractive girl friend, and this led the Barker boys to figure they were missing a good thing. Soon Freddie, Dock and Karpis had their "molls" accompanying them. Ma Barker objected. She had always preached against the "wickedness" of liquor and women, but now her influence was waning.

The gang decided to try more sophisticated crimes and on June 15, 1933, kidnapped wealthy St. Paul brewer William A. Hamm. Negotiations were conducted successfully, and his family paid a ransom of a hundred thousand dollars. He was released unharmed.

News of the Hamm kidnapping broke at the same time as another sickening slaughter. FBI agents had arrested Nash in Hot Springs, Arkansas, and returned him to

Kansas for trial for the Cloud County Bank robbery. As agents and police, seven in all, got off the train at Kansas City, Pretty Boy Floyd and other hoods, armed with sub-machine guns, opened fire. Nash was killed—but so were three police officers and an agent. The nation was shocked. The "Kansas City Massacre," together with the kidnapping of Hamm, spurred Congress to action. Bills were introduced to permit the FBI to make arrests and to carry weapons. When this legislation was passed and went into effect in 1934, the days of the Barker-Karpis gangsters were numbered.

They were hardly aware of it. After the Hamm kidnapping, they robbed a bank in South St. Paul, killing one police officer and crippling another. In Chicago they killed another officer in a getaway from a minor holdup. In January, 1934, the gang kidnapped Edward G. Brenner, a bank president, and after holding him for three weeks, collected two hundred thousand dollars in ransom.

These events put a tremendous strain on the FBI, for they coincided with robberies and murders committed by Dillinger, Floyd, Nelson and others. The 325 FBI agents were spread pitifully thin, being shot at, ridiculed and flouted. Yet Hoover and his men were learning new techniques. A key one was constant pressure. Wherever the Barker-Karpis gang went, Hoover's men were close behind. They permitted them no rest and no safety.

Hoover formed a Special Squad to track down the Midwestern gangs. He took personal charge in Washington, coordinating the activities of agents in a score of investigations in a dozen states and sending men where they were needed most. State lines melted away as the FBI developed mobility and means of communication exceeding anything the gangs could muster.

Hoover's men used what has been called a "scorched earth" policy in chasing the criminals. They wanted Ma Barker and her sons Dock and Freddie. They wanted Karpis, Dillinger, Nelson, Floyd and Kelly, but they arrested whomever they could find—girl friends, the doctors who bandaged their wounds, the "fences" who handled their stolen property, the mechanics who fixed their cars, the men who sold them guns or ammunition—anyone and everyone who aided or abetted them in any way. Slowly the sources of supplies dried up. The gangs ran out of people to help them.

Hoover used publicity as a crime-fighting weapon as police had never done before. The photographs of wanted men were everywhere in newspapers and in movie newsreels. Millions of Americans could identify them instantly. Every move they made was blared from the radio. They were labeled as "Public Enemy Number One" or "Public Rat Number One," and the entire nation was put to looking for them. Hoover and his agents became heroes as public opinion swung to their side.

Finally, Hoover used his crime lab to turn the hoodlums' slightest mistakes into evidence that could be used against them. The kidnappers of Brenner the banker were identified from a single fingerprint of Dock Barker found on a can used to fill the gas tank of the getaway car. Four flashlights used to signal the ransom payoff were traced to a St. Louis store, where the salesgirl identified the purchaser as Alvin Karpis.

Pressure, publicity and scientific evidence forced the gang to go into deep hiding in widely separated areas. Dock Barker and two other members of the gang underwent excruciatingly painful "operations" to have their faces and fingerprints changed, but to no avail. On January 8, 1935, agents traced Dock Barker through a girl friend and arrested him in Chicago. Other members of the gang were arrested nearby, and one, Russell Gibson, chose a shootout with agents. He figured a bulletproof vest would save him, but he fatally underestimated the marksmanship of the newly-armed FBI men. From Gibson and Dock Barker, agents collected an arsenal of automatic weapons.

In Dock's apartment agents found a map of Florida with circles around Ocala and Lake Weir. This tied in with other information Hoover had, and about five-thirty on the morning of January 16, 1935, agents crept close to a lakeside cottage. Agent-in-charge E. J. Connelley hollered, "We are special agents of the Federal Bureau of Investigation. I'm talking to you, Kate Barker, and you, Fred Barker. Come out one at a time and with your hands up."

About fifteen minutes elapsed. The command was repeated, only this time Connelley threatened to use tear gas to force them out.

Ma Barker shouted, "All right, go ahead!" A submachine gun spoke from the house, spraying the area near Connelley. Agents fired back with machine guns, shotguns, rifles. For four hours the battle raged, creating a din usually heard only at a war front. Finally, there was silence from inside the cottage. Agents crept close and found Ma Barker dead, a shroud of tear gas around her, a machine gun in her left hand. Freddie lay dead beside her. Inside the cottage were two sub-machine guns, two shotguns, two automatics, two rifles, with ample ammunition for all.

The death of Barker and his mother, the capture of Dock, left only Al Karpis at large. In fact, only Karpis remained of the entire Midwestern hoodlum empire. Dillinger was killed in July, 1934, in Chicago. In October of that year, "Pretty Boy" Floyd pulled his last trigger as Hoover's men cornered and killed him. Nelson went down in his last shootout in November, but took two agents with him.

Only Karpis remained, and he was to write a strange chapter in Hoover's life, providing one of the most nefarious moments in the history of law enforcement.

After Ma Barker's death, Karpis and his pal, Fred Hunter, scooted from Miami to Atlantic City, New Jersey. They again got in a gun battle with police and fled, this time to Toledo, Ohio. On April 24, 1935, they robbed a mail truck in Warren, Ohio, of seventy thousand dollars and then a train of thirty thousand dollars, escaping by airplane—a new tactic in the old art of the getaway.

On June 5, 1935, Karpis and Hunter landed in Hot Springs, Arkansas, long a favorite "vacation spot" for criminals. It was easy to see why. Hot Springs was in those days "wide open," with gambling, prostitution and assorted other forms of vice. Police neither saw, heard nor spoke of this evil, and high-ranking police officers were known to be more than tolerant of well-heeled hoods—if the price was right.

Karpis and Hunter had the proper price, so they enjoyed several months in Hot Springs. They drove a car stolen in Ohio and parked it on Main Street, while Karpis made a liaison with the madame of the biggest bawdy

house in town, among whose regular customers were the
chief of detectives and chief of police. These officers
never saw Karpis' wanted posters, although they were
plastered all over the police station.

In March, 1936, this travesty of law enforcement
ended when irate citizens of the town notified the FBI
that they believed Karpis was there. When agents arrived, they found that Karpis and Hunter had fled. Eventually the Hot Springs chief of police, chief of detectives and chief identification officer were tried and convicted of harboring criminals, largely on testimony produced by the FBI.

Karpis remained Number One on the Most Wanted
List. More than that, he was Number One on Hoover's
personal list. Hoover had drummed into his men that
teamwork was everything. There were no heroes, no
stars, no rugged individualists in the FBI. The team was
everything—but Karpis was an exception. Hoover wanted
him personally. Instructions were sent out to notify him
any time agents got any information on Karpis. Thus,
Hoover had been standing by at the airport in Washington ready to fly to Hot Springs to arrest Karpis, but
he had been disappointed. Hoover continued to bide his
time.

In April Hoover went to Capitol Hill to appear before
the Senate Appropriations Subcommittee that was con-

sidering the FBI's budget. Although he had been on the job a dozen years by then, Hoover was still only forty-one years old. Tennessee's Senator K. D. McKellar challenged Hoover's age, background and experience in the field of criminal investigation and dwelt on the fact he had never arrested a criminal.

Hoover said nothing, but his face was flushed with rage. He felt his personal courage had been questioned in public, that he was being accused of asking his men to face dangers he would not face himself. More than ever he was determined to arrest Karpis—personally.

His chance came on April 30. Agents trailed Karpis and Hunter to New Orleans and then to Florida and Texas and now back to New Orleans, where they were holed up in a Canal Street apartment. Hoover raced there by plane.

A small army of agents joined him, surrounding the house. Hoover put men on the roof, men on the fire escape, men at the back door. Next he arranged that as soon as he and three other agents started from the corner in their car, all the other men were to move in. It had been carefully rehearsed—and it promptly fell apart as Karpis and Hunter came out of the house and got in their car.

Hoover ordered his driver to step on the gas and intercept the Karpis vehicle before it left the curb. But at that moment a mounted policeman, ignorant of the drama unfolding, came down the street on a big white horse. Hoover had to wait till he passed. Not knowing what was going on, the officer might have started shooting agents instead of crooks. The cop passed, and the Hoover car started forward. But a child on a bicycle came by. Again Hoover had to wait. He couldn't risk a child, even to get Karpis.

Finally the coast was clear and Hoover raced up and snatching open the door to Karpis' car, arrested Public Enemy Number One before he had a chance to draw his gun.

"All right, boys, put the cuffs on him," said Hoover.

What cuffs? Not one agent had a pair of handcuffs on him, hardly a reflection of their confidence in their leader. Since a crowd was gathering and Hoover wanted to get Karpis and Hunter out of there, he ordered them bound with neckties and put in Hoover's car.

"To the Post Office Building," Hoover barked.

Where was that? The agent behind the wheel was from Oklahoma and had never been in New Orleans in his life. He hadn't the faintest notion where the Post Office was.

"Mr. Hoover," broke in Karpis, "if you mean the new Post Office, I know where that is, because I was just goin' to rob it."

Fortunately Hoover meant the *old* Post Office, which

they reached after obtaining directions from a passing pedestrian. Hoover later noted the pedestrian "probably would have died" had he known Public Enemy Number One was there, bound with the necktie of FBI Agent Number One.

J. Edgar Hoover is perhaps not a detective in the classic sense of a Goron, Neil or Pinkerton. He is seldom personally present to hunt for clues, interrogate suspects, make arrests and testify in court. He is more an organizer, administrator, and inspirational leader of such detectives.

Yet Hoover is perhaps the first of a new breed of detective who combats crime as one of a team, using the best of laboratory science, communications, transportation and brains. Hoover's personal contribution toward development of these new techniques is beyond measure. That he is in his forty-second year as FBI director is ample testimony to his worth.

RAYMOND
CAMPBELL
SCHINDLER

Protector of the innocent

† The girl sitting in the leather chair in a plush Manhattan office was nineteen years old and extremely attractive. She was also sobbing almost uncontrollably. Finally, she got herself under control and said: "If you will save my husband from being hanged as the murderer of my father, I will pay you all the money you may ask."

That was a most generous offer, for the girl was Nancy Oakes, oldest daughter of Sir Harry Oakes, often called the "Midas of the Bahamas," a rather fitting description of a man who owned the fabulous Lake Shore gold mine in Canada and a fortune estimated at two hundred million dollars. He had been found cruelly slain in his bed in Nassau two days before, and the following day Nancy's husband, Count Alfred de Marigny, had been arrested and charged with his murder.

In the desperate situation of having her father, whom she loved, murdered, and her husband, whom she also loved, in danger of hanging for it, Nancy Oakes de Marigny turned to the man she believed best able to help her, Raymond Campbell Schindler, American private investigator and one of the great detectives of all time.

In 1943 Schindler was sixty-one years old and at the apex of a distinguished career. He had hurried to New York from the West Coast just to see Nancy Oakes and learn of this fascinating murder in the Caribbean paradise. As she spoke, he observed her intently and was impressed with her youth, gentleness, shyness—and courage. She was moving forthrightly to defend her husband, a much-maligned man who, overnight, had become the popular choice for the murderer. The case was a sensation, even shoving news of World War II off the front pages of newspapers. Nonetheless, this girl, shy or no, was propelling herself into the midst of this sensationalism in order to help her husband.

So, impressed by her, Schindler listened, then fixing his pale blue eyes on her, said, "I will do my best, my dear, but on one condition. If my investigation turns up evidence your husband is guilty, I will turn that evidence over to the prosecution."

She blanched and nodded. "But I tell you, Mr. Schindler, my husband is not a murderer."

Ray Schindler, so short and fat he resembled an egg, flamboyant, often unpredictable, yet a man some considered the greatest detective of his time, thus entered one of history's most bizarre murders, an apparently senseless crime, carmarked by a weird combination of imponderables and improbables.

Schindler was born in Mexico, New York, on November 11, 1882. His father was a Universalist minister and moved his family first to Oswego, New York, then to Marshalltown, Iowa, and to Whitewater, Wisconsin. In 1900, when he was eighteen, Schindler went to California, investing his savings in a gold mine. He lost it all and by 1906 was penniless.

On April 19, 1906, the day after the great earthquake and fire, he arrived in San Francisco and answered an ad for a "historian." This turned out to be insurance investigating. He was to prove San Francisco properties were destroyed by the earthquake, an act of God for which no damages were paid, rather than the fire, for which policy holders could make claims.

Schindler did excellent work that brought him to the attention of Hiram W. Johnson, a leading attorney who later became California Governor and U. S. Senator. About this time, William J. Burns, the famed Secret Service agent, came to San Francisco to investigate graft in the city government and, at Johnson's recommendation, hired the young Schindler as his assistant. In 1909 Burns left the government and opened his celebrated detective agency, taking Schindler with him as manager of the main office in New York. Three years later Schindler opened his own agency.

The Schindler Detective Agency grew to be one of the largest in the world, largely on the basis of Ray Schindler's talents. In "brain power" he was generally considered to be a notch or two above all other "private eyes." He was exceedingly thorough, particularly in the use of scientific means of detection, by which he solved some sensational cases. He grew wealthy and famous, but he continued to help the poor as well as the rich. And he always insisted on finding out the truth about the case, not just whether a person was guilty or innocent.

All of these qualities Schindler took with him to Nassau. They would be needed, for a nearly hopeless task lay before him. The government of the Bahamas, a British colony, had an airtight case against "Freddie" de Marigny. There was no love lost between the murdered man and his son-in-law. They had quarreled bitterly in public. De Marigny could not account for his time when the murder was committed, and he even admitted to being within a block of Westbourne, the fifteen-room beach house where Oakes' life was taken. The suspect could not find the clothing he had worn the night of the murder, and there was evidence the hair on his face and arms had been singed—most incriminating, since there had been a fire in the murder room. Worst of all, one of De Marigny's fingerprints was found at the scene. To ask Schindler to find this man innocent was to ask him to work a miracle.

Schindler landed at Nassau on the twelfth of July, four days after the murder. From the beginning he found Nassau authorities hostile. He was followed day and night. Everyone he questioned was interrogated immediately afterward by police to determine what he had learned. He was refused access to files, to information, to witnesses. Schindler quickly discovered that Nassau officialdom wanted not so much to discover who murdered Oakes as to prove that his son-in-law did it.

Gradually Schindler pieced together the essential facts of the case. Sir Harry Oakes was alone in Nassau while his wife and children were summering in Maine. The night before the murder, he had some friends into Westbourne, and one of them, Harold Christie, had spent the night, sleeping in the bedroom next to Oakes. The rooms were connected by a common bath and dressing room, and both opened onto the same balcony, where the two men planned to meet at 7 A.M. for breakfast. When Oakes failed to join him, Christie went to his room. As soon as the door was opened, smoke belched out. Christie screamed, "Harry! For God's sake!"

The fire had largely destroyed the mattress, bed and area around it. Oakes lay diagonally across the bed. Parts of his body, including his face and especially his eyes, were cruelly burned. Feathers from a pillow had adhered to the seared flesh.

It was not the fire that killed him, however. He had been bludgeoned to death by a "blunt instrument." There was much blood over the bed. It was obvious that whoever had killed Oakes had started the fire to destroy the evidence, figuring the flames would destroy the entire house. But he had mistakenly left an electric fan running at the foot of the bed, and it had blown out the flames, leaving the smoking, smoldering fire which Christie discovered.

Schindler also learned that the investigation of the murder had been flawed from the inception. For one thing, the murder had gone unreported for over three hours. Christie had become hysterical and done several irrational things. He had tried to "revive" Oakes by pouring water down his throat. Then, having moved the body and gotten covered with blood, he had made several phone calls from the bedroom, smearing blood over the phone and the phone book while looking up numbers. The calls were made to Christie's brother and other individuals from whom he sought advice. Finally, police were called.

Governor of the Bahamas at the time was the Duke of Windsor, the King who had given up the throne of England to marry an American divorcée. In his official capacity he now took actions which greatly affected the case. Instead of relying on Bahamian police, who were quite competent, he called in outside help—and not Scotland Yard or the Federal Bureau of Investigation. He invited in Captain Edward Melchen of the Miami, Florida, police. Melchen had once served as the Duke's bodyguard during a visit to Florida, and the Duke placed great confidence in him. Melchen flew to Nassau in great haste, bringing with him Captain James O. Barker, supervisor of the Miami Crime Laboratory. It was he who discovered the print from De Marigny's little finger, right hand, on a Chinese screen that had been near Oakes' bed.

With characteristic thoroughness, Schindler investigated the people involved in the case. Sir Harry Oakes was a surveyor's son, born in Sangerville, Maine, in 1874 and educated at Bowdoin College. When gold was discovered in the Klondike in 1896, he went to Alaska and spent thirteen years in a vain search for it. Then, booted off a train in Ontario because he lacked money for a ticket, he was befriended by a Chinese restaurant owner who loaned him money to invest in a nearby mine. Gold was discovered, and Oakes staked a claim to the fabulous Lake Shore Mine, estimated to have yielded two hundred million dollars.

Oakes made money in nearly every endeavor after that and amassed one of the world's great fortunes. In 1923 he married and settled down in the Bahamas, largely to escape income taxes, but maintained palatial homes in many lands. His many charities won him a knighthood in 1939. At the time of his murder he was known as a gruff, often uncouth man, accustomed to having his own way. He was widely respected and admired, yet he had many enemies.

Schindler discovered that Oakes had been acting strangely of late. It was as though he were afraid. He had even started sleeping at Westbourne, rather than his main house, and he kept a gun in his nightstand. This weapon, unfired, was found the morning after the murder, but police had not kept it as evidence, a fact Schindler thought most strange.

Count Alfred de Marigny was everybody's choice for the murderer. He was invariably depicted by reporters who flooded into Nassau as a foppish, idle, ne'er-do-well playboy, who flashed a phony title and married Nancy

Oakes—she was his third wife—just for her money. Oakes supposedly had objected to the marriage, but she had run away with De Marigny the day after her eighteenth birthday. Oakes thus hated his son-in-law, and they quarreled bitterly.

Schindler, with characteristic independence, refused to accept the public's view of De Marigny and made his own investigation—with surprising results. De Marigny was of French ethnic origins but held English citizenship. He was a legitimate count, but seldom used the title, even on official papers. Rather it was his wives who were fascinated to be called countess.

Far from being idle, De Marigny had a degree in agricultural science and was a successful poultry farmer and businessman. Although not nearly so wealthy as Oakes— who was?—he was moderately successful and had refused offers of aid from his father-in-law. Nancy had similarly refused help from her father.

Not unlike Oakes, De Marigny was an outspoken man who preferred the company of men to women and felt uncomfortable in formal situations. He was a yachtsman of note, an outdoorsman and a self-made man. These qualities rather appealed to Oakes, as did the fact De Marigny was not afraid of him. Rather than animosity, there was a sort of grudging respect and an uneasy truce between the two men. They fought, for both were strong-willed men, but Schindler could find no deep-seated hatred likely to produce premeditated murder.

The detective pursued De Marigny's activities on the night of the murder. He learned that the Count had been at his cottage some five miles from Westbourne—Nancy was attending dance classes in Vermont. There had been a noisy party at the cottage, attended by, among others, De Marigny's closest friend, George de Visdelou and his sultry sixteen-year-old girl friend. Originally De Marigny had planned an outdoor party but moved it indoors when a storm arose. The lights had gone out and, in lighting hurricane lamps, De Marigny had singed his arm and the small Vandyke beard he had recently grown.

About 1 A.M., as his party was breaking up, De Marigny drove two women guests to their homes. This drive took him past Westbourne, which was dark by this time. He returned immediately to his cottage, said goodnight to George de Visdelou and his girl friend, and went to bed. Later, De Visdelou took his girl home and returned to spend the night with De Marigny. He parked his car behind De Marigny's and—his keys in his pocket—went to bed.

The prosecution maintained that De Marigny then left his house, drove to Westbourne, clubbed Oakes to death, disposed of his blood-stained clothing so it could not be found, and went back to bed. To Schindler this was patently impossible. To do that, De Marigny would have had to go up to De Visdelou's room, obtain his keys and back De Visdelou's car out, take his own car to Westbourne, park it in his drive, and return De Visdelou's car and keys to their original locations, all without waking his guests, all on a stormy night when almost no one in Nassau slept soundly.

Was it possible that De Marigny left his cottage during the time De Visdelou was taking his girl friend home? Schindler drove from the cottage to the Oakes house repeatedly in all kinds of weather and decided it was possible for De Marigny to have made the trip in the allotted time. He might even have clubbed his father-in-law on the head and gotten back. But set the fire? Never.

Schindler proved this by obtaining samples of the clothing, bedding and carpets—the Nassau authorities had not taken Schindler's interest in these matters seriously—and proved that the quickest this material could have burned was in forty-five minutes. Other evidence showed Oakes had been killed out of bed and carried to the bed after the fire was started. Furthermore, from the position of the feathers on the body, Schindler was able to deduce that they could not have been blown over the body by the fan, but must have been sprinkled over the body by hand.

All of this evidence led Schindler to the conviction the

murderer must have lingered at the scene close to an hour after the murder had been committed, setting the fire, burning out the dead man's eyes and mutilating other parts of the body, and spreading feathers over the remains. Thus, it was apparent to Schindler that De Marigny could not possibly have committed the murder in the time allotted him.

Rather—and this intrigued Schindler greatly—the crime had many aspects of a ritualistic voodoo murder. It was an idea he was never able to get out of his head, or to prove.

Schindler was shocked and appalled at the investigation made by the Nassau police and the Miami detectives. No proper autopsy was ever performed. The body was hustled aboard a plane for the U.S. where it was to be buried, and then the plane was recalled so detectives could take pictures as evidence. No X-rays were made of the skull to determine what weapons inflicted the four triangular-shaped depressions in the skull. Police said a wooden picket was used, a convenient explanation since such stakes were on the property. Schindler established that no wooden picket could be driven with such force into the skull. The murder weapon was never found, nor was it ever agreed what sort of weapon might have been used.

Furthermore, doctors found a strange black fluid in

Oakes' stomach. No attempt was made to analyze or identify it.

There were guards on duty at the estate, but police did
not question them. They were allowed to melt into the
native population, so Schindler could not find them. A
mysterious boat had been seen mooring in the vicinity of
Westbourne and men from it going ashore. No effort was
made to identify them. A reliable witness swore he saw
Christie in town at the very time he claimed to be sleeping undisturbed while the murder took place and a fire
was started in the adjoining bedroom.

But it was the conduct of the investigation inside the
murder room that astounded Schindler. The room had
been invaded by all sorts of people after the murder, so
that it abounded with fingerprints. The Chinese screen
on which De Marigny's print was supposedly found was
actually picked up and carried out into the hallway before
it was analyzed for prints.

Although Captain Barker was thought of as a fingerprint expert, whole sections of the room were never
dusted for prints. The furniture, walls, doorknobs and
much else were covered with bloodstains. There were
whole, bloody handprints on the walls, and the blood was
never analyzed to see if it was Oakes'. The bloody fingerprints were ruined forever by Barker, who dusted them
while they were still wet.

Perhaps the most damning evidence of official neglect came when Schindler asked authorities why the bloody handprints were not analyzed and received this reply: "The fingers were stubby and De Marigny's were not, so we dismissed them."

This determined effort to convict De Marigny while ignoring all evidence that might prove his innocence led Schindler to say, "I shall never understand how an honest investigator could have permitted this to happen. In my opinion, it is criminal negligence."

The most incriminating evidence against De Marigny was the fingerprint which Captain Barker said he had lifted from the wooden frame of the Chinese screen. That in itself was strange. One of the rules of evidence is that prints are lifted—that is, dusted with powder and removed from the surface with tape so that the outline of the print remains intact—only from objects that are immovable. The screen was hardly that. It was, in fact, brought into court as evidence.

Barker had taken no pictures of the print on the screen, again a rudimentary procedure. In fact, Schindler discovered, Barker had not brought his fingerprint camera with him, assuming he would use that of the Nassau police. But their camera was broken, so Barker took no photographs of the vital print. Schindler, with his usual thoroughness, learned that Barker made no effort to send for a camera or to use the Royal Air Force camera available in Nassau.

This was, however, so much nitpicking, for there could be no denying that the print was that of Alfred de Marigny. It was the one incontrovertible piece of evidence that would hang the Frenchman.

From the moment he entered the case, Schindler questioned the fingerprint. He brought in a leading American expert, Maurice O'Neill of New Orleans, and together they examined the print. It had a background of circles beneath the print, which puzzled them.

Schindler and O'Neill went to work on the Chinese screen. They lifted every print and analyzed it. This was a laborious task taking several weeks, for there were hundreds of prints on the wood. Not one single print presented the background of circles. There were wood grain marks, as would be expected, but not circles. Schindler and O'Neill tried to produce a print that duplicated the circled background and, after weeks of effort, gave up. It was impossible.

Finally, they turned to the exact spot where the incriminating print was supposedly found. They tried, tried, tried—and failed, not only to produce the strange print, but to produce any fingerprint at all that could be lifted!

To Schindler there was only one possible conclusion

Incredibly, Captain Barker was lying about that print.

But it was not enough to prove to himself or even to defense counsel Sir Godfrey Higgs that De Marigny was innocent. Schindler had to convince a jury, and that was not easy. Feeling was running high against the French count. At one time it had been feared he would be taken from his cell and lynched by a mob. In the fever of newspaper sensationalism in which the investigation was conducted, it was hard for any person to remain objective.

The trial began on October 18, and Schindler's work played a prominent role. He produced an elaborate and exact scale model of De Marigny's car, driveway, and the two vehicles which demonstrated most graphically that the defendant could not have moved the cars without awakening the neighborhood.

Captain Melchen, the Miami detective, found his testimony undermined when he took the stand. Each point of neglect in the investigation was brought out and dramatically hammered home to the jury.

Then began the three-day cross examination of Captain Barker. As it turned out, both he and his testimony were destroyed, as he was inundated with evidence he could not have lifted the print from the screen. His professional competence impugned, his integrity questioned, he could only admit lamely that he wasn't sure where he found the print.

The emotional climax of the trial was the testimony of Nancy Oakes on behalf of Alfred de Marigny. The sight of the grieving girl defending her husband won over the most doubting Thomas.

When the jury found De Marigny innocent, the courtroom erupted into shouts, and he was carried outside to freedom on the shoulders of the spectators.

In the years that followed, tragedy befell many of the participants in the case. Captain Melchen died in bed. Captain Barker became a drug addict and in 1952 was shot and killed by his own son, a crime which was adjudged self-defense and never prosecuted. Lady Oakes continued to be harassed by letters and phone calls from cranks offering to solve the case.

De Marigny was deported from the Bahamas, itself a great injustice. He had no more than reached Cuba than two attempts were made on his life. His marriage to Nancy Oakes could not survive the strain of events, and it was annulled in 1949. For a time he was a man without a country, but eventually he was admitted to the United States. He remarried there and ultimately settled down to a quiet life in South America.

Schindler tried several times to convince Nassau authorities to reopen the investigation. He said he felt he knew who had killed Oakes and could prove it, if given a chance. Others have thought the same, but Bahamian police continue adamant and the case remains closed—to the satisfaction of no one. Even today, speculation about Oakes' murderer is a popular subject of conversation in Nassau.

Ray Schindler died on July 1, 1959, at his home in Tarrytown, N. Y., a widely respected and extravagantly admired detective. But the greatest accolade came from Erle Stanley Gardner, the attorney and celebrated author of mystery stories:

"The fact the fingerprint, unquestionably that of De Marigny's little finger, authenticated by police testimony as being on that wooden screen, didn't put the noose right around De Marigny's neck is one of the greatest investigative triumphs of modern times. I know of no detective who has ever faced a tougher assignment or discharged it more triumphantly."

ROBERT
FABIAN

Policeman with a
thousand questions

† A fragile sun was breaking wanly through the overcast as a car nosed into the curb in front of Jay's jewelers in London's West End. Three men, masked with scarves, ran inside. Guns were drawn, and one bandit vaulted the counter while a second barked, "This is a holdup!"

But Jay's Jewelry Store was not to be robbed that afternoon. Alfred Ernest Stock, sixty, a director of the firm, slammed the big safe door shut—and for his action was pistol whipped to unconsciousness by one of the bandits. The store manager, Bertram Thomas Keates, seventy, was ordered to open the safe. His reply was to heave a heavy wooden stool at the gunman, who ducked and fired at the same time. The bullet missed Keates and thudded into the shop wall. Soon other clerks were rushing up, and the would-be bandits turned tail and ran.

Out in the street more trouble developed. Their car was blocked by a truck, so they ran on foot, still masked, still clutching guns. It made a wild scene, and pedestrians, screaming, scurried for cover.

All but one. Alex de Antiquis, father of six children, came by on his motorcycle. He saw the trio, sped after them and, just as he came abreast, turned off the engine of his motorcycle and skidded it right into their path. They jumped over and around it, and one instinctively fired a shot. The bullet struck Antiquis in the left temple between the ear and eyebrow. He toppled into the gutter, mortally wounded.

That attempted robbery and murder in 1947 brought to the scene one of Scotland Yard's most respected detectives, Robert Fabian, who would soon become superintendent of the Yard. He was in fact acting superintendent this day, while his superior was on vacation.

Born in 1901, Fabian started out in life to be an engineer, like his father. He did not do well in his studies, however, and appeared headed for a career as a draftsman. But, not liking the long hours cooped up indoors, he joined the Metropolitan Police in 1921. After two years as a uniformed man, he became a detective.

In the years which followed, Fabian had a dozen celebrated cases, but his fame came to rest largely on the case of the Piccadilly bombs. In June, 1939, Irish extremists set off a bomb—a popular pastime then—in crowded Piccadilly Circus. Fabian was one of the first detectives to arrive, but even then he had to elbow through a large crowd to reach the scene.

It was nearly midnight, fortunately, so no one was injured in the blast. But several shops were badly damaged. Broken glass was strewn over the sidewalk, along with rubble from the shop windows. Fabian later described his first action this way: "We have a saying in the Metropolitan Force: 'Give your eyes a chance.' I stood there in the heart of this hubbub and let my eyes roam."

What he saw numbed him with fear—a parcel, partially hidden, wrapped in brown paper. He stooped to examine it, saw the adhesive tape binding it, and felt it. Hot! Another bomb!

Fabian shouted to other police to get the crowd back and to bring a fire bucket so he could douse the bomb. But there was no bucket. "Somebody needed to do something quickly," recalled Fabian some time later, "and with a strange lonely dread I realized that it was up to me to do it."

Carefully, as hundreds watched, he unwrapped the lethal package and removed, one by one, sure each movement would be his last, ten four-ounce sticks of gelignite, a powerful explosive—forty ounces in all. In one a fuse was stuck. Fabian removed the fuse with his pocket knife —later learning that the knife blade scraping against the grit in the gelignite could have set it off. Blissfully ignorant, he hacked up all ten pieces to make certain there were no hidden detonators.

Fabian's alertness and bravery had saved perhaps a hundred lives that night. He was awarded two medals, one for gallantry by the King at Buckingham Palace, the other a suitably inscribed bronze medal by the West End underworld, who figured Fabian had saved some of their lives, too.

As long as there is a Scotland Yard, Robert Fabian's disarming the bomb on the public street will be part of its lore. But the murder of Alex de Antiquis posed a different type of challenge.

In a way it was a typical police case. The crime happened quickly and without warning. A carelessly planned and executed robbery turned into murder. Fabian foresaw a quick solution. He had an abundance of evidence: a stolen car parked in front of the jewelry shop; a bullet in the woodwork; a bullet in the murdered man's head; a revolver abandoned at the scene; and no less than 27 men and women who had witnessed the shooting. An easy case.

One common misconception is that all a detective has to do is discover clues, figure out their meaning and arrest the culprit. A lot more than clues is needed, as the Antiquis murder soon proved.

The first bad news came from Fred Cherrill, superintendent of the Fingerprint Department. His men had gone over the stolen car and the interior of the shop. They had found a lot of prints and lifted many of them, but not one could be used to identify a suspect. Next came the report of the crime lab. The car, a stolen Vauxhall, had been examined carefully for hairs, fibers, stains, anything that would identify its most recent occupants. Result: zero.

Dr. Bernard Spilsbury was called in to make an autopsy. Antiquis had died of a gunshot wound, all right, but that was all the useful information he could develop. The ballistics lab, with the celebrated Robert Churchill doing the work himself, concluded that the murder bullet was fired from a .32 caliber revolver, but not the one abandoned at the murder scene. The bullet in the woodwork of the store was from a third gun.

Fabian's confidence in the simplicity of his case began to wane rapidly as one after another of Scotland Yard's best scientific crime labs, perusing the abundance of "clues," found nothing that identified the murderers or even told Fabian where to start looking for them.

There were still the twenty-seven eyewitnesses. One of them must have seen something. The interrogations were carefully conducted and produced results beyond belief:

"Three enormous men . . ."

"Three dodgy little fellows . . ."

"I think one was lame . . ."

"They all ran like blazes . . ."

"All wearing raincoats . . ."

"They wore battledress jackets . . ."

"Definitely foreigners, swarthy . . ."

"They were blond and wore no hats . . ."

"Caps pulled down over their eyes . . ."

The descriptions were impossible. The witnesses in the excitement of the events had seen what they wanted to see or, having no idea what they had seen, had made up the whole tale.

Fabian worked totally without sleep for the fifty-five hours which immediately followed the murder—and had his case collapse around him. A world of clues he had, and now he didn't even know where to begin looking for a suspect.

Then he got his first break—without which few difficult cases can be solved. A taxi driver named Albert Victor Grubb came forward to say that shortly after the murder a young man with a handkerchief knotted under his chin had jumped on the running board of his cab. Since he already had a fare, Grubb pushed the fellow off. He ran to the door of Brook House, Number 191, Tottenham Court Road, where another young man was standing in the doorway. Both went inside.

At dawn Fabian was at the door of Brook House waiting to talk to Leonard Joel, the porter. Informed of what the taxi driver had seen, Joel exclaimed, "Yes, yes, that might account for the key I found when I swept the stairs yesterday."

"What key?" Fabian asked.

"I just told you, Inspector, the key I found on the stairs. And don't ask me if it belonged to anybody in the offices—I done asked them all."

"Where is the key now?"

Triumphantly, as though retrieving a Crown jewel, the janitor reached in his pocket. "Right here."

Fabian snatched it and sent one of his men to try it in the ignition of the stolen Vauxhall. Back came the marvelous words, "It fits, Chief. It fits!"

Now the entire attention of Scotland Yard centered on Brian Cox, an awestruck young office boy who had been standing in the doorway when the two men brushed past him and hurried into the building. Cox said the tallest of the strangers wore a raincoat. After a while he met them on the stairs. "Mr. Williams in?" asked one. Cox said he didn't know any Mr. Williams.

Fabian got one useful piece of information from Cox. The tall man who had worn the raincoat into the building didn't have it on when Cox saw him later on the stairway. A search was begun of the office building and in an unused room on the top floor, Fabian found a bundle shoved out of sight behind a dusty counter. In it was the raincoat with a cap and gloves in the pocket. Underneath the bundle was a crumpled scarf, folded into a triangle and knotted at both ends—the murder mask.

The label had been ripped from the coat in an effort to render it unidentifiable. But Fabian was an expert on tailoring. He tore out the coat lining and, as he figured he would, found a stock ticket inside the seam near the right-hand pocket. This label showed the coat to be a popular brand of ready-made clothes.

The crime lab examined the coat, cap and scarf, finding nothing, so Fabian sent men to Leeds, the city where the coat had been manufactured. They came back with the news the raincoat had been delivered to one of three stores in London.

Grimly, Fabian and his men pursued this clue. The first tailor shop produced the names and addresses of several people who had bought a similar coat. Detectives called at each purchaser's home to ask if he still had the raincoat. Each did. The pattern was repeated at the second store. Again a great deal of leg work—for nothing. Finally, they went to the third store and got an address of an apartment in Bermondsey. It was the last hope.

Fabian himself knocked at the door. A woman answered. "Does this belong to your husband?" Fabian asked, showing her the raincoat.

She seemed surprised. "Why, yes. He lost it in a pub."

"How long ago, ma'am?"

"Oh, I'd say about five weeks ago."

Fabian thanked her and left, weary and discouraged. All this effort for a blind alley—a stolen raincoat devoid of clues. But, since he had one minuscule chance left, he assigned a detective to watch the flat in Bermondsey.

Fabian had hardly returned to his office when the woman walked to an apartment a few blocks away, stayed briefly, then returned home. A quick check developed that she had visited a family named Jenkins, the eldest son of which was at that time serving eight years for manslaughter committed during a robbery of a London jewelry store. Another son, Harry Jenkins, had recently been released from Borstal Prison.

As Fabian pondered this development, he was presented with a new one. A schoolboy found a gun, fully loaded but with one chamber fired, in the mud of the river Thames. Ballistics examined the gun and pronounced it to be the murder weapon. Fabian sighed in resignation. It would have been too easy to have found the gun on a suspect.

A few minutes later Fabian's office door opened and detectives ushered in the man who lived in the Bermondsey flat. Fabian had stationed his men so as to intercept him before he arrived home and talked to his wife. Now Fabian showed him the raincoat.

"Yes, that's mine," he said. "I lost it at the cinema a few weeks ago."

Fabian smiled. "Your wife said you lost it in a pub. Who's making the mistake?"

He hesitated, then sighed. "We both are. She loaned it to her brother, Harry Jenkins."

Harry Jenkins, arrested and brought before Fabian, turned out to be handsome, cocky and tough. Before he was twenty, he had two convictions for assaulting policemen, having broken the jaw of one. Now Fabian showed him the raincoat and said, quietly, "I understand you borrowed it from your sister's husband."

Jenkins looked Fabian in the eye and smiled cockily, "It looks like that coat," he said—but not one other word. He was jailed.

A list of Jenkins' associates was drawn up. Two names stood out, Christopher James Geraghty, twenty-one, who had twice escaped from Borstal Prison, and Terence Peter

Rolt, seventeen, who had been arrested for shoplifting. Rolt was picked up first—and released, when he said he was home in bed, ill, on the day of the shooting. Geraghty appeared voluntarily at Fabian's office. Asked about his activities on April 29, he replied, "As a matter of fact, I was in bed. I had some boils and was ill all week." He, too, was released.

An hour later Jenkins was put in a line-up. Fabian saw that he knew all the tricks, such as sticking a newspaper in his pocket. Witnesses seeing this figured he had just come in off the street and therefore couldn't be the suspect.

For one hour and twenty-seven minutes the witnesses who had claimed they could identify, without fail, any of the three gunmen who had slain Antiquis, stared at Jenkins. Not one picked him out. But Fabian was not discouraged. The longer Jenkins went unidentified, the more he was convinced he was the leader of the gang which had murdered Antiquis.

The line-up over, Fabian sent for Jenkins and saw the brazenness in his eye. He knew Jenkins was daring him to try to pin anything on him—and knew he could not. All he could do was shrug and sigh, "All right, Jenkins. You can go."

Detectives following Jenkins, Geraghty and Rolt soon had a reunion, for the three suspects met at a restaurant, where they appeared nervous, apprehensive and talked in whispers.

Fabian had run his slender clue of the raincoat as far as it would go, so he now undertook to use other methods to solve the case. He asked Jenkins and his sister to come to the station, ostensibly to make a formal statement about the raincoat. Actually the detective wanted to study the two of them together.

But it was Fabian who was surprised as Jenkins said, "I want to tell you who I loaned the raincoat to." He not only named the individual, one Bill Walsh, but virtually told where he could be found.

Obviously, Fabian thought, Jenkins had decided to solve the case for Scotland Yard. And an appealing solution it was. Bill Walsh was an ex-convict known to the Yard and a parole violator already being sought. If police nabbed him, they would be only too glad to blame him for the Antiquis murder and remove it from the list of unsolved crimes—or so Jenkins figured.

Along with two men Fabian went to Southend, where Jenkins indicated Walsh could be found. They remained in the police station drinking tea and studying the bulky Occurrences Book. This is a record of all the happenings in the station area. All the seemingly meaningless reports, complaints, phone calls, interrogations, and street incidents are recorded in the Occurrences Book.

Going through it was a painstaking process—but rewarding. Four days before the murder a patrolman had discovered two young men acting suspiciously in a phone booth. He'd taken their names as Christopher James Geraghty and Michael Joseph Gillam. How interesting, Fabian thought.

Now the detective went in search of Bill Walsh. Jenkins had said Walsh was running around with a waitress at a Southend café. After much leg work, Fabian found her, then went to speak to her father.

"Yes, Bill Walsh was in Southend on April 25," said the father. "He was here with Harry Jenkins. But that was the last we saw him."

"Have you seen Jenkins since then?" Fabian asked.

"Sure, I seen him."

"Did you ask him about Walsh?"

"I did. He said Walsh had double-crossed him. He was going to get his revenge, he said."

To Fabian this set of seemingly unrelated events could only mean that Walsh and Jenkins had pulled a robbery on the night of April 25 and that Walsh had run off with the loot. Had Jenkins' revenge been to finger his erstwhile compatriot for the Antiquis murder?

For the rest of the day Fabian and his men searched the homes of Walsh's known friends. A most careful search it was, and it paid off. They discovered two

watches stolen in the holdup of a jewelry shop in Queensway, London—on the night of April 25.

A full-scale search for Walsh was initiated. After three
days, he was found and brought into Fabian's office. Was
this the murderer? At thirty-seven, he appeared too ludicrous to be one, resembling in his padded pinstripe suit a
character from a Humphrey Bogart movie. Yet he was a
man in deep trouble, and he knew it. Fabian did nothing
to ease his mind when he said, "Walsh, you are wanted
for parole violation and maybe for armed robbery—and
perhaps for murder. It depends on what you have to tell
us."

Walsh blanched and hesitated and lit a cigarette and
paced the floor and lit another cigarette and asked for
water, which was given him. Fabian sat quietly, a tomcat
waiting for a cornered rat to choose which of several
equally undesirable holes he was going to run through.

Walsh first denied he had ever borrowed any raincoat
—particularly *that* raincoat—from Jenkins or his sister.
Walsh was vehement in his denial and Fabian believed
him.

After much soul-searching and many agonized sighs,
Walsh admitted he knew of the holdup of Jay's in which
Antiquis was killed. He, Jenkins, Christopher Geraghty
and a fourth fellow who later withdrew from the scheme
had planned the robbery. Walsh had even reconnoitered

the shop five days before the robbery. "But," pleaded Walsh, "I was not one of the guys who did it. I swear I wasn't, Inspector. You gotta believe me."

Fabian peered at him intently and said, so softly his words were barely audible, "You would make it much easier to believe you if you told me about the robbery at Queensway."

Walsh's distress was great. He was down to two last holes—murder or robbery. He chose the lesser offense, admitting that along with Jenkins, Geraghty and a fellow he knew only as "Joe," he had robbed the Queensway shop of rings and watches worth five thousand pounds.

Then Fabian, his face a mask of ignorance, said, "You split the loot three ways, of course."

Walsh hemmed, hawed, then said, "No, I took the whole swag and beat it."

Fabian believed Walsh and rewarded his truthfulness by charging him with the Queensway robbery—along with Joe. The Occurrences Book had revealed who Joe was—Geraghty's companion in the phone booth, Michael Joseph Gillman.

As interrogation of Walsh was taking place, the second missing gun was found in the Thames mud not far from where the first gun was discovered. This second gun was established to be the one that put the slug in the wall of the jewelry shop.

Of more interest to Fabian was the fact both guns were found less than a quarter mile from the home of Jenkins' wife.

The clue of the raincoat had gone a long way and Jenkins, unintentionally to be sure, had been most helpful in solving the Queensway robbery. But what of the murder? Fabian knew he could question Jenkins till doomsday and get nowhere. So he had Geraghty picked up. Fabian talked to him quietly, almost fatherly, sizing him up, probing for a weak spot.

The detective discovered that, at the merest mention of Jenkins, Geraghty bristled and clammed up. Obviously, he and Jenkins, both inmates at Borstal Prison, were prepared to die for each other. Geraghty would say nothing about his friend. So Fabian asked him about Rolt.

Geraghty poured out a Niagara of words about Rolt, a young, teenage punk who meant nothing to him. He gave a long, detailed statement in which he implicated himself and Rolt, but spoke only of "that other fellow whose name I don't want to mention." Fabian let him tell about the events at Jay's perpetrated by himself, Rolt and "that other fellow."

As described by Geraghty, they had broken into a gunsmith's on Saturday and stolen the guns and ammunition. On Tuesday they inspected several jewelry stores around the Tottenham Court Road area, deciding to rob Jay's. By this time it was noon, so while Geraghty and "that other fellow" had lunch, Rolt was sent to study the window at Jay's. He came back with a report that it was worth about two thousand pounds. Geraghty later inspected the window and upped the estimate to five thousand pounds. Meanwhile Rolt and "that other fellow" stole the Vauxhall.

The robbery was planned for Rolt to remain in the car while the more experienced Geraghty and "that other fellow" did the job. But—and Geraghty told it quite indignantly—Rolt, the fool, had jumped out of the car, pulled his gun and, when the going got rough, started to shoot. There was nothing to do but run. When Antiquis appeared, Geraghty had no choice but to shoot him.

Fabian arrested Rolt at his home at two-thirty in the morning, telling him that Geraghty had made a statement that named him. Crying like a child, Rolt sobbed out his story and signed a statement. His story was similar in every detail to Geraghty's except "that other fellow" became, as Fabian expected, Harry Jenkins.

Rolt, as a minor, got life. Jenkins and Geraghty were hanged. And Inspector Robert Fabian closed one of his most famous investigations.

UNITED STATES
BUREAU OF NARCOTICS

 |||||

A smooth-working team

† Is the "master detective" a thing of the past?

There is some evidence he is. One is hard pressed to think of a present-day master sleuth like Neil or Fabian or Goron, or even Irey. And yet major crimes are committed almost daily—the theft of gems from the Museum of Natural History in New York, for example, or the slaying of civil rights workers in Mississippi. A dozen more come to mind. These cases are solved; in fact, a much higher percentage of cases is solved than ever before in history. Why then are there no master detectives?

One reason is that we are simply less aware of individual detectives. We are less naive. A half-century of violence, war and crime has jaded our sense of injustice and our judgment of the sensational. A trunk murder, the gunning down of a pedestrian, even a massacre of several people tend to be old-hat—or quickly superseded by a more heinous deed.

Another reason for the seeming shortage of master detectives is that today's detective is a team man, working with a ballistics expert, toxologist, pathologist and others. Instead of following a clue, today's detective will often phone or radio information to his headquarters, where another detective will pursue the lead or interrogate the suspect or make the arrest. Each detective's work is diluted by the work of his teammates. He becomes faceless. He cannot point to major cases he alone has "solved."

The dilution of individual effort is increased because solution of crime involves multiple jurisdictions these days. Rare is the important crime that does not involve two or three police departments, state troopers and one or more federal law enforcement agencies.

Another reason the master detective has "disappeared" is because of the complexity of police work. Police forces have grown to such size—over twenty-six thousand in New York City—that the simple administration of them is a full-time job. In 1890, Goron, as head of the Sûreté, could spend weeks solving the Gouffé case, and twenty years ago Fabian could give a great deal of attention to the Antiquis murder. Today this is impossible. A large city force, the FBI, or postal inspectors or Treasury agents have a dozen, perhaps a hundred major cases going on at one time, all crying for attention. It would be highly unlikely today for Hoover to take the time to arrest a criminal like Karpis.

Under today's system the man who is a good detective is promoted and promoted again, each time taking responsibility for more and more men and additional investigations. The higher his rank, the more he is a supervisor, the less a detective.

The role of the detective has changed, too, because the nature of crime has changed. An increasing amount of crime is perpetrated by young people. The detective finds himself playing the role not only of sleuth but of psychologist, sociologist, occupational therapist and babysitter. He may spend more time trying to "solve" the underlying social causes of crime than crime itself.

There are still plenty of grown-up murders, robberies, extortions and other crimes committed by individuals or small gangs of men who figure they can outsmart the law. As serious as such crime is and as time-consuming as it is for detectives, it is hardly the most serious today. Far more serious are crimes spawned by international narcotics smuggling rings or crime syndicates which control gambling, vice, narcotics and other activities that are illegal and profitable.

The really serious crimes today are not, as they used to be, murder and robbery. Today's racketeers and gangsters have learned their lessons from Capone. They avoid violence whenever possible. They pay their taxes. They mock their illegal activities by operating legitimately in real estate, construction, trucking, unions, wholesale foodstuffs and clothing and a dozen other areas.

To fight these criminals, a "master detective" working alone is not enough. What is needed is a national crime-fighting organization that uses the talents of hundreds, thousands of detectives and other law enforcement men.

Today's detective is certainly not inferior to his historical forebears. But he is better organized. Are there master detectives today? Yes, hundreds of them. They are nameless, faceless, dedicated, unappreciated. How they operate is demonstrated by the following case from the files of the United States Bureau of Narcotics.

As Salvador Pardo-Bolland stalked through the Nice Airport on the French Riviera on February 14, 1964, his manner was that of a banker attending a convention of paupers. He was imperious, impeccable from the mirror shine on his shoes to the Homburg precisely angled on his graying hair, utterly the man of distinction. When he beckoned a porter to follow him, it was an invitation to make a salaam.

As if leading an entourage, Pardo-Bolland marched to the baggage checkroom, where he presented claim checks for four large suitcases. When these were set out, the awed porter leaped to take them. He grabbed two of the bags, intending to put them under his arm. But they were deceptively heavy and he almost dropped one.

"Careful, you fool!" barked Pardo-Bolland. "Don't drop it."

With profuse apologies and a new respect for the weight of the luggage, the porter carefully placed them on a handcart and transferred them to the scales at the ticket counter. Pardo-Bolland tipped the porter and paid for his ticket, including sixty pounds of excess weight. After receiving profuse bows and bountiful expressions of "Merci, Monsieur Ambassadeur," he took his seat in the first class cabin. Even there he acted like a maharaja among the untouchables.

All this was carefully and clandestinely observed by U. S. narcotics agent Al Garafalo, who was certain he was witnessing the start of another run by the "Striped Pants Express"—the name given to diplomats who abused their diplomatic immunity by smuggling a wide variety of contraband into the U. S.

In this case, Garafalo believed Pardo-Bolland, Mexico's Ambassador to Bolivia, was lugging as much as a hundred pounds of pure heroin, enough of the juice of degeneracy to stock all the addicts in the United States for weeks. When "cut" with lactose and sold by pushers, it would be worth ten million dollars.

Garafalo's observation of Pardo-Bolland was quickly relayed to the Bureau of Narcotics in Washington, where agent Andy Tartaglino read the report with satisfaction. The big fish was approaching the net.

Tartaglino knew almost precisely what Garafalo had seen at Nice Airport, for he had been a U. S. narcotics agent in the South of France a half decade before, when the Striped Pants Express had first been derailed. A tall, handsome man who looked more like a gondolier than a cop, Tartaglino had learned in the late 1950's that most of the heroin shipped into the U. S. came from a band of Corsicans. They ran a sort of merry-go-round of narcotics production. Opium was grown legally in Turkey, converted to morphine base and illegally smuggled into Marseilles. There, using German scientists, the Corsicans refined it into pure heroin and shipped it to their U. S. cousins, the Mafia—via the Striped Pants Express.

Using diplomats as smugglers was pure genius. The world over, they are treated with the utmost courtesy. They are whisked through customs without even cursory inspection. They are immune from arrest. A diplomat doesn't even get a traffic ticket, so who is to stop him from smuggling dope?

For almost ten years no one did. Then, in 1960, Tartaglino learned that Mauricio Rosal, Guatemalan envoy to the Low Countries, was involved in the smuggling operation. Rosal, his Corsican contact and an airline purser were nabbed in New York in October, 1960, along with 220 pounds of heroin. It was the largest haul of "junk" ever made in this country. Agents were delighted. They had broken an international dope ring and ruined a new method of smuggling. Diplomats could no longer break laws at will and claim immunity.

In the next few months, Tartaglino and other agents who had worked so hard on the Rosal case began to learn the dismal truth. The price of junk, which had leaped after Rosal's arrest, was down again, indicating heroin was once more plentiful. How had another source of supply been developed so quickly? The answer was learned in prison. The airline purser talked. So did a big trafficker arrested in Canada. Both gave the same fact: Rosal was only one smuggler. There was another diplomat carrying heroin.

Another diplomat. It was like looking for a match in a conflagration. On any given day there are hundreds of diplomats in New York. They come from 113 nations which send delegations to the United Nations and maintain embassies in Washington and consulates in various cities. What's more, New York is a stopover point for diplomats traveling to and from Latin America, Asia, Africa and Europe. Any one of them could have a suitcase full of heroin. And the Corsicans, once burned by Rosal's arrest, would not be so careless again. The task of finding the new diplomat-smuggler was virtually hopeless.

Fortunately, Tartaglino and other U. S. agents got an assist from the Sûreté. The French detectives found Gilbert Coscia living in Cannes on the Riviera under an assumed name. As Tartaglino, who eagerly reported this fact to his superiors in Washington, knew, Coscia might not be *the* boss of the Corsicans, but he would do till a bigger one came along. He had gone into hiding after Rosal's arrest, and only months later, in early 1961, had he been located.

Rather than arrest Coscia, the Sûreté tailed him—and Coscia failed to spot the tail. Every move the squat, watery-eyed hood made was observed, including his frequent meetings with Juan-Baptiste Giocobetti, another well-known French crook. Every piece of mail was recorded. Every phone call to and from Coscia's home had an audience. In this way, the French police discovered that Coscia frequently received cryptic cablegrams from various points around the world, including New York,

Montreal, Mexico City, even the UN. The cables would bear such messages as "Richard Arrived Safely."

Coscia was also a traveling man, making frequent trips to Montreal from France. On four occasions he also made short trips to New York from Montreal.

With this information the task of finding the ambassadorial accomplice of Coscia became possible—but certainly not easy. Since the dates of Coscia's entry into New York were known, the agents could concentrate on those diplomats who were in the city on those same dates and pick out the one most likely to be carrying heroin.

But there were thousands of diplomats traveling to New York on the four dates when agents knew Coscia had been there. To find out which one was *the* diplomat, agent Andy Tartaglino was brought back to the U.S. He was a marvelous choice for a number of reasons. He was a sort of walking encyclopedia of the French narcotics racket in general and the Corsicans in particular. He could draw on his years in the South of France—hopefully—to spot some diplomat who was a frequent visitor to the Riviera and just happened to be in New York with Coscia. More than knowledge and experience, he had desire. Helping to catch another diplomat would be a big boost to his career. But beyond that, he simply wanted to catch the smuggler. The thought of a hotshot ambassador being kowtowed to and receiving special privileges while carting in junk angered Tartaglino. How nice to help the ambassador exchange his striped pants for a prison uniform.

Tartaglino and agent Ken Sawyer, who was assigned to help him, started out hoping for luck. They hoped Coscia would have been dumb enough to travel in the same plane as the diplomatic courier. He wasn't. They hoped a name would stand out among the travel manifests as an obvious suspect. None did. Luck or no luck, the job was done anyway. The agents studied hundreds, then thousands, tens of thousands and hundreds of thousands of travel manifests. They computed lists of every diplomatic traveler who arrived or departed New York before, during or after Coscia's four visits. They listed the diplomats by country and position and checked out their reason for being in New York. Did the diplomats have legitimate affairs in the city? Or were they just passing through? Did they have criminal records? Was there some link, no matter how tenuous, which tied them to the Mafia or the Corsicans, to narcotics or to smuggling?

Tartaglino and Sawyer checked over *one million* manifests. It took them three years, but they found their man, a slim, handsome man in his fifties with an aquiline nose, aristocratic face and plenty of brains—Pardo-Bolland. He had a Doctor of Laws degree and had practiced as an attorney before joining the Mexican Foreign Service in

1930. He had served posts in Latin America, Europe, the Middle East and Asia before being named, in 1959, Mexico's Ambassador to Bolivia. Travel manifests pointed to Pardo-Bolland and no other. Furthermore, he had been in the various cities when cablegrams were sent to Coscia. Still, Tartaglino couldn't be sure. Pardo-Bolland seemed too smart and aristocratic to try smuggling. He had connections—and an American wife. He couldn't be a dope carrier—or could he?

The facts were gone over again. All evidence continued to point to Pardo-Bolland, but in this game there wasn't room for mistakes. If U.S. narcotics agents arrested the wrong man, it would create an international incident, provide new fuel for the "Hate America" campaign. Congressmen would make speeches and launch investigations. Agents' careers would go down the drain. So Pardo-Bolland was investigated further. He had, Tartaglino and Sawyer learned, an abiding admiration for money and, apparently, a total disinterest in how he got it—as long as he wasn't caught. The decision was made. Pardo-Bolland went under surveillance.

With the selection of the Mexican as the likely suspect, the Narcotics Bureau readied its forces to trap him. Tartaglino was brought into Washington to coordinate the case. Over him was George H. Gaffney, the agent who had arrested Rosal in New York and had risen to Deputy

Commissioner, and Henry J. Giordano, who had cracked many a top case on his way to becoming Commissioner. He knew catching Pardo-Bolland and the Corsicans would not be a one-man or even one-nation show. Lots of teamwork would be needed, particularly with the French. Thus, the best possible liaison was established with Commissioner Charles Guillard, the crack investigator who headed the Narcotics Bureau of the Sûreté.

By the end of 1963, all was in readiness in Washington and Paris to derail the diplomatic express. Coscia and Giocobetti were being watched, and Pardo-Bolland couldn't make a move without the agents knowing about it. Or so it was thought.

On Thursday, February 6, 1964, Pardo-Bolland, while "holidaying" in Europe, traveled by train from Holland to Paris—and quickly lost his tail. Embarrassed French police frantically raced around to Paris hotels shoving pictures of the balding diplomat under the noses of room clerks. Finally, they found Pardo-Bolland registered under the name of Suarez de Mendoza. To Tartaglino this meant the Mexican wasn't using his diplomatic immunity at this stage of the game. It also meant he was a smart and cautious man and that he wasn't in Paris to pick up pastries.

On Friday, Saturday and Sunday, Pardo-Bolland, whose tastes in entertainment ran to girlie movies, became an inveterate church-goer. He visited shrines and cathedrals all over Paris. He'd stop in front of a church, light a cigarette, wait awhile, then go inside. After kneeling a few moments, he'd come out, walk to another church and repeat the scene. This ecclesiastical merry-go-round ran all weekend—but in one of those pews Pardo-Bolland picked up his instructions. To agents following him, it was obvious that Pardo-Bolland was super-cautious and scared of being caught. Narcotics agents have a word for it: Pardo-Bolland was "hinkty."

On Monday, the tenth, he flew from Orly Airport outside Paris to Nice, where he registered at a hotel, again as Suarez de Mendoza. In Nice he came under the surveillance of Agent Garafalo, who felt certain Pardo-Bolland was there to pick up the heroin. He was willing to bet that when the Ambassador left Nice his luggage would weigh considerably more than when he had arrived. Garafalo checked with the airline. On the flight in, Pardo-Bolland had carried two suitcases weighing twenty-five kilos or about fifty-five pounds.

On Tuesday, Pardo-Bolland went to the railroad station in Nice to meet an incoming passenger. The new fellow was middle-aged, just under six feet tall and strapping. He was balding, sharp-nosed, afflicted with immense ears and clearly a man who carried himself well. He was also a total stranger, and Garafalo looked to the

French detectives for help in identification. They could only shrug.

While an urgent call went out to Tartaglino in Washington and Commissioner Guillard in Paris for identification of the newcomer, Garafalo followed him and Pardo-Bolland. The pair rented a car and drove to Cannes, where they met with two men who needed no introduction—Coscia and Giocobetti.

During the next two days the foursome met frequently, giving agents time to identify the large-eared man as Juan Arizti, a *Ministerio de Ralaciones Exteriores* of the government of Uruguay. Another diplomat! Further information was that he lived in Montevideo with his wife and child, that he was in Europe for his health and that he was rumored to be the next Uruguayan ambassador to Moscow. Very interesting, but Garafalo wanted to know what Arizti was doing in Nice. Was he going to carry junk? Or was he there as a smokescreen for Pardo-Bolland?

In Washington, Tartaglino fretted over the new development. This Arizti character was a total, absolute shocker. Tartaglino had no information or even indication *another* diplomat might be involved. The whole thing could be just a coincidence. Pardo-Bolland was the one they were after. He had to be.

On Friday, the fourteenth, Pardo-Bolland checked out of his hotel, motored to the Nice airport and boarded a flight for Paris. Sure enough, just as Garafalo had predicted, Pardo-Bolland's luggage had doubled, both in number and in weight. He phoned Paris. Agents would renew the tail as soon as Pardo-Bolland landed.

Arizti remained in Nice, as did Garafalo. On the next day, however, Arizti got up in the morning, paid his hotel bill, summoned a cab and hied off to the airport. Like an imperial personage, he stalked through the terminal, retrieved two suitcases and four black valises from the baggage claim room and got on a plane for Paris. Garafalo looked on in astonishment. What was this guy up to? Whatever it was, Garafalo knew he'd better stay with him and hastily booked passage on the same plane.

Meanwhile, the agents who were tailing Pardo-Bolland the day before had been treated to a round of dirty movies when the Mexican went into Paris. Arizti followed a different course. He remained at Orly only an hour, long enough to change planes for a jet flight to Montreal. A puzzled Garafalo went along.

To Tartaglino the case was a mystery—and an alarming one. Were they going to be led on a chase all over the world? Was Arizti a decoy? Or were both diplomats carrying heroin? Tartaglino's eyes brightened. What a haul that would be. A hurried call was made to the Royal Canadian Mounties in Montreal to join the chase.

On Sunday, the sixteenth, Pardo-Bolland suddenly reversed his field and took off from Orly for New York, carrying his weighty suitcases. Tartaglino informed U. S. customs men, New York City police and authorities at Kennedy International Airport. All of these groups joined the U. S. narcotics agents, the French Sûreté and the Royal Canadian Mounties in an international, intercontinental game of hide-and-seek with two diplomats, a Mexican and a Uruguayan, both, either or neither of whom might be carrying narcotics.

Arizti landed at Montreal, explaining to customs men that he had come for his health and a rest. He piled his luggage into a taxi and went directly to the railroad station where he stashed his four black bags in a locker. Mounties followed him for the next three days as he, too, suddenly turned devout. He rubber-necked at every church of note in Montreal. Meanwhile, Mounties sought to satisfy their curiosity—and everyone else's—about Arizti's role in the dope-running scheme. His locker was opened and the four black bags examined. They contained packet after packet of pure, high-grain heroin, 135 pounds of it, worth $13.5 million. The stakes of the game had suddenly been raised.

Pardo-Bolland landed at Kennedy Airport right on schedule and was met by some very slick agents. They slid him through customs and slipped him into a government-owned undercover taxi—but only after marking his suitcases as the ones he had brought into the country.

"Where to, mister?" asked the agent posing as a cabby.

"The Elysée Hotel."

"The Elysée Hotel. Yessir." These words were picked up by agents posing as porters while they stuffed Pardo-Bolland's luggage into the taxi. The name of the hotel was then flashed by radio to George Belk, who headed the Narcotics Office in New York. He dispatched men to the hotel to arrange to have Pardo-Bolland placed next to a vacant room—into which were carried some of the most sensitive electronic listening devices made by man.

As the cab took off for Manhattan, the driver maintained a steady line of chatter, drawing out of Pardo-Bolland that he had been a former swimming champ— and was vain as a peacock.

Pardo-Bolland arrived at his hotel and checked into his room—carrying his bags with him. The groan was heard all the way to Washington and Paris. Tartaglino, Belk, everyone working on the case had hoped to open the Mexican's luggage to see what he was carrying. If he'd checked them, they could have inspected them. Now they couldn't. From Washington had come strict orders against making illegal searches that could cause an international incident or jeopardize a conviction.

That Pardo-Bolland kept his bags with him would just make life harder for agents. New York is so big and so crowded it is difficult to follow a man there. Pardo-Bolland could hop a taxi carrying those bags and lose his tail in a minute. He could get rid of the dope, pick up his money and all the effort would have been wasted. So the order went out not to lose Pardo-Bolland. Teams of men were set up to keep him in view at all times. In between tricks, agents could relax—if that were possible —in rooms 4923 and 4925 at the Americana Hotel.

On the evening of Monday, the seventeenth, Arizti, tailed by Mounties, went to the railroad station in Montreal and, still bearing himself regally, picked up the four black bags and boarded the train for New York. When he arrived at Pennsylvania Station the next morning, he was met by an agent disguised as a redcap, who helped him deposit the bags with another agent in the baggage claim room. Arizti was handed claim checks Numbers A226453 through A226456. As far as Arizti was concerned, those four pieces of paper laid claim to $13.5 million. He quickly hailed a taxi—the undercover one—

and was whisked to the Hotel Élysée, where agents were able to put him into a bugged room.

From then on both Pardo-Bolland and Arizti were within sight or earshot or both. And it was all legal. There was no telephone tap. No entry was made into their hotel rooms. Agents sitting in adjacent rooms used devices which enabled them to hear a whisper through the wall. When the diplomats met in a bar or restaurant, agents were nearby.

To Tartaglino and to Gaffney and Giordano looking over his shoulder, it was a case of so-far-so-good. The diplomats had landed safely and were still not wise to the trap. Arizti had stashed his heroin. Obviously, the claim checks would be turned over to a Corsican representative who would, in turn, deliver them to a Mafia man in the U.S. Sooner or later someone would claim those bags and take them somewhere. All the agents had to do was wait—and not make these fellows any more hinkty than they were already. Now, if they only knew what Pardo-Bolland was going to do with his stuff.

On the afternoon of the eighteenth, shortly after he conferred with Arizti, Pardo-Bolland went to the Hotel Americana and asked for a Monsieur Blanc.

"What was the name, sir?" the room clerk asked.

"Blanc. Monsieur Blanc."

"Is that B-l-a-n-k?"

"No, no, no! B-l-a-n-c. Blanc."

"Just one moment, sir." Shortly the clerk returned. "I'm sorry. We have no B-l-a-n-c registered here."

Pardo-Bolland's annoyance mounted. "But you must have. Look again."

"I'm sorry, sir, we have—"

"*Es Stupido!* I insist there is a Monsieur Blanc registered here. In fact I am certain of it." By his manner, Pardo-Bolland might have been an agitated Attila exhorting his Huns to sack Rome.

"I'll check again, sir." In two minutes the clerk returned. "I'm sorry, but there positively is no Monsieur Blanc registered here. Perhaps you have the wrong hotel."

The finality of the clerk's words seemed to sink in, and Pardo-Bolland visibly wilted. "Perhaps I do," he said meekly. As if to prove it to himself, he went to the Hotel St. Moritz to inquire for Monsieur Blanc, but he wasn't there either. Greatly disturbed, Pardo-Bolland returned to his hotel.

Agents followed Pardo-Bolland's plight with great glee, for in the machinations of international smuggling, he had committed a goof comparable to going off without his pants. He had the wrong name for his contact in New York. He and Arizti were stuck with umpteen million dollars' worth of heroin and no one to give it to.

The diplomats had only one way out. They cabled Carmen Lopez the code name used by the Corsicans, at a post office box in Cannes. It read: "Cousin is not found at indicated address." It was signed: Richard Bernard.

Nothing happened all day on the nineteenth, except for the mounting nervousness of Pardo-Bolland and Arizti, whose imperiousness was melting like a snowstorm in his native Montevideo. Then, shortly after midnight on the twentieth, Pardo-Bolland received a transatlantic phone call. Since they did not tap the phone, agents could hear only Pardo-Bolland's words: "Oh, Leroux—Americana. I have it." Obviously, he had been set straight on the contact's name.

At 8:00 A.M. on the twentieth, Pardo-Bolland left the Hotel Élysée and went to a pay phone on the street, dialed the Americana, asked for Leroux and talked briefly. Then he headed for the Americana, tail in tow. Since he now had the room number, he didn't bother the room clerk. Straight to the elevators he went, pushed the button for the forty-ninth floor, rode up, got out and headed down the hall. At a hotel room door, he stopped, knocked and entered—to the total consternation of the agent who trailed him—room 4924.

Of all the hotel rooms in the city of New York, the long-sought contact with the Corsicans had all this time been in one right across the hall from the off-duty lounge of the agents. They remembered the short, swarthy Frenchman. They recalled riding up and down the elevator with him and even sitting next to him in the hotel bar. But what they couldn't remember was whether they had said anything to give themselves away.

Pardo-Bolland stayed in room 4924 only two minutes. Not long after he left, Leroux departed, too. If he knew where he was going, he was the only one. He went over Manhattan as if surveying it for resale to the Indians. By foot, taxi, bus and subway he traveled, avoiding only the hansom cabs. Clearly Leroux knew all the tricks for shaking a tail. He wasn't missing one.

Agents were not shaken, though, but was that good? Had he spotted them? That evening, when he tossed the keys to the valises into a public trash can on the street, it seemed that he knew he was being followed. Or did he simply get rid of the keys because they weren't needed? The bags could be opened without keys. Agents worried and tension mounted.

While this was happening in New York, events were taking place across the Atlantic which vitally affected the case. For over three years the Sûreté had successfully maintained surveillance on Coscia, yet sometime on the twentieth he learned he was being watched. The vast

international network working against the smuggling
ring was finally toppled by some well-bribed informer.
Coscia ran—and fast. He got out of his house, out of
Cannes, out of France to Geneva, Switzerland, before
the Sûreté knew he had even stirred.

Coscia's speed was provoked in large part by his desperation. It was painfully obvious to him that if the
Sûreté had been trailing him, they knew of his shipment
and of his meeting with Pardo-Bolland and Arizti. The
Americans must be in on it, too. He must stop the trans-
action in New York before the Mafia was lured into a
trap.

That night, shortly after he arrived in Geneva, Coscia
phoned New York twice, talking to Leroux and to Arizti.
Agents heard the phone ring in the Uruguayan's room
and listened to his Spanish expletives. Then he burst into
Pardo-Bolland's room and blurted: "They're wise to us.
We got to get out." The frustration in Washington was
boundless. Thanks to the delay caused by the confusion
in names, the case had blown up in their faces.

The following morning, the twenty-first, the two diplomats ran around Manhattan trying to book a seat on
the first available flight out of the country. Any flight
would do. Any destination would be fine.

Leroux also visited airline offices, but limited himself

to Swissair, where he made reservations on a 7:30 P.M. flight that night for Geneva.

He walked out of Swissair on Fifth Avenue, down a block and across the street. That's where the agents took him. Just as they closed in, Leroux dropped the baggage claim checks, but he was spotted doing it. At 2:35 P.M., Arizti and Pardo-Bolland were arrested in their rooms at the Élysée.

Pardo-Bolland's luggage was seized and opened on the spot. There was no dope in the suitcases. Pardo-Bolland hadn't been smuggling. He had been the decoy for Arizti. The haughty Mexican triumphantly wrapped himself in his diplomatic immunity like a shroud.

A few hours later in Los Angeles, when President Lyndon B. Johnson sat down for a previously scheduled conference with Mexican President Lopez Mateos, he told him of his ambassador's arrest, describing the conspiracy and Pardo-Bolland's involvement. Mateos disowned Pardo-Bolland on the spot, thus relieving him of his immunity. The Uruguayan government did the same to Arizti. Both men had forgotten that immunity is granted a government, not individuals employed by it.

Both Arizti and Pardo-Bolland pleaded innocent at their trials. The Mexican was belligerent. He was just an innocent ambassador minding his own business. His luggage contained no narcotics. He knew nothing of heroin, smuggling, Corsicans or the rest of this nonsense.

"Why didn't you go on to your own country?" Prosecutor William Tendy asked him.

"I wanted some medicine."

"What medicine?"

He said a word which sounded like "veeks."

"Would you spell that please?"

"V-i-c-k-s."

"Would you show the court which medicine you obtained."

Pardo-Bolland left the stand, went to his confiscated luggage and presented to Tendy, as if it were a precious Aztec relic, a small green and yellow box containing good, old-fashioned, therapeutic cough drops.

Arizti took another tack at his trial. Yes, he had carried the four black bags into the country. Yes, he had done all those things. But he didn't know about the heroin. Pardo-Bolland had come to him and said, "Amigo, I have some extra luggage. Since you're going to New York, would you mind terribly carrying it for me?" Obliging to a fault, Arizti had accommodated his friend.

Even the tight-lipped René Bruchon—Leroux's correct name—had to shake his head when he heard that whopper. But maybe the yarn helped. Arizti got only ten years, compared to eighteen for Pardo-Bolland and fifteen for Bruchon.

Arizti's simpleton story is more easily understood when you realize he was still quivering from his close call. Agents explained to him that when the Mounties opened the four black bags in the Montreal Railway Station, they, as well as U. S. agents, decided that all the heroin the bags contained could not be allowed into the country.

So they had substituted flour for the heroin, leaving only a quarter kilo in each bag to incriminate Arizti. "Except for that small amount," Arizti was told, "all you carried into the country, worrying every step of the way, was 134 pounds of flour from the sergeant's mess at the Royal Canadian Mounted Police barracks in Montreal."

As Arizti blanched, an attempt was made to console him. "But look at how lucky you are we arrested you. If you had turned over all that flour to the Mafia, how long do you suppose you would have lived?"

ROBERT LISTON grew up in Ohio and graduated from Hyram College there. He came to New York to be a writer, and for a while, he says, "starved and wrote little." During the Korean War he edited a frontline newspaper and discovered in himself a real love for journalism. After the war he joined the staff of the Baltimore *News American* and specialized for eight years in reporting major crime stories. He has since been a freelance magazine writer, and his work has appeared in *True, Saturday Evening Post, Reader's Digest* and *Life*. He has also written three other books for young readers, including *Your Career in Law Enforcement*.

Mr. Liston lives with his wife and three children on the shores of a woodland pond in Westport, Connecticut, where he swims and ice-skates when not at his typewriter.